ALSO BY EDWARD W. SAID

Joseph Conrad and the Fiction of Autobiography

Beginnings: Intention and Method

Orientalism

The Question of Palestine

Covering Islam

Literature and Society (editor)

The World, the Text, and the Critic

After the Last Sky (with Jean Mohr)

Blaming the Victims (editor)

Musical Elaborations

Culture and Imperialism

The Politics of Dispossession

Representations of the Intellectual

Peace and Its Discontents

The Pen and the Sword

Entre guerre et paix

Henry James: Complete Stories, 1884–1891 (editor)

Out of Place: A Memoir

The End of the Peace Process

The Edward Said Reader

Reflections on Exile and Other Essays

Power, Politics, and Culture: Interviews with Edward W. Said

Parallels and Paradoxes: Explorations in Music and Society
(with Daniel Barenboim)

Humanism and Democratic Criticism

From Oslo to Iraq and the Road Map

ON
LATE
STYLE

ON
LATE
STYLE

Music and Literature
Against the Grain

EDWARD W. SAID

Foreword by Mariam C. Said
Introduction by Michael Wood

PANTHEON BOOKS, NEW YORK

Three of the essays in this book were originally delivered, in slightly
different form, as Northcliffe Lectures, and several essays originally
appeared, in slightly different form, in *Grand Street, London Review of
Books, The Nation,* and *Raritan.*

Pantheon Books and colophon are registered trademarks of
Random House, Inc.

Library of Congress Cataloging-in-Publication Data

Said, Edward W.
On late style : music and literature against the grain / Edward W. Said ;
foreword by Mariam C. Said ; introduction by Michael Wood.
p.   cm.
Includes index.
ISBN 0-375-42105-X
1. Creation (Literary, artistic, etc.) 2. Artists—Psychology.
3. Arts, Modern—Philosophy. I. Title.

NX160.S25 2006   700'.1'9—dc22   2005051029

www.pantheonbooks.com

Printed in the United States of America
First Edition
2   4   6   8   9   7   5   3   1

CONTENTS

FOREWORD

Edward was in the process of writing this book when he passed away on Thursday morning, September 25, 2003.

In late August we were in Europe: first in Seville, where Edward participated in the West Eastern Divan workshop, and then in Portugal visiting friends, when he fell ill. We returned to New York a few days later, and after three weeks of high fever he began to pull through. He felt well enough to resume work Friday morning, three days before his illness took over for the last time. He said to me as we were having breakfast that morning, "Today I will write the acknowledgments and preface to *Humanism and Democratic Criticism* (the last book he finished, which was about to come out). The introduction to *From Oslo to Iraq and the Road Map* I'll finish by Sunday. And next week I'll concentrate on completing *Late Style,* which will be finished in December." All this was not meant to be. However, Edward left us a tremendous amount of material on this book to allow us to finish it and produce posthumously a version of what he had in mind.

My recollection is that this idea—writers', musicians', and other artists' "late works," "late style," "Adorno and lateness," etc.—became part of Edward's conversation sometime at the end of the 1980s. He had begun to be interested in this phenomenon and was engrossed in reading about it. He discussed it with many friends and colleagues and began to include examples of late works in many of his articles on music and literature. He even wrote specific essays on the late works of some writers and composers. He also gave a series of lectures on "late style," first at Columbia and then elsewhere, and in the early 1990s he taught a class on the topic. Finally he decided to write a book and had a contract in hand.

This book would not have been possible without the help of several devoted people and friends. My family and I are more than indebted to them for their contribution toward this endeavor.

Our thanks first and foremost go to Sandra Fahy, Edward's assistant, whose help and dedication were crucial in assembling the material that went into this book. We are also grateful to Andrew Rubin, Edward's student and former assistant, who kept detailed notes, was very resourceful, and directed us to various valuable sources of information. And to Stathis Gourgouris—who had long discussions on late style with Edward—for his valuable time and willingness to share his ideas. To Shelley Wanger, Edward's editor, whose patience and perseverance we will always cherish, to Sarah Chalfant and Jin Auh at the Wylie Agency, and to Akeel Bilgrami, Edward's friend and colleague, who taught several seminars with him and who read the manuscript—to all of them go our heartfelt thanks. I also would like to thank the many friends and former students contacted who were very helpful with their time and information. Last but not least, this book would not have seen the light of day without two dear friends to whom my family and I are most grateful and will always be indebted for their love, generosity, and expertise. The person whose wisdom, advice, and meticulous reading of the material gave us the green light to proceed with this publication was "America's finest literary critic," as Edward always described his friend Richard Poirier. Richard oversaw this manuscript from beginning to end. The other person who labored on and edited this manuscript with a fine-tooth comb and devotion is our close friend Michael Wood. He has done a superb job of not only editing the essays and arranging the material, but also putting it all together without losing Edward's voice.

Mariam C. Said
New York, April 2005

INTRODUCTION

"Death has not required us to keep a day free,"[1] Samuel Beckett writes with grim and intricate irony, suggesting both that death doesn't make appointments and that we can die just as well when we're busy. But death does sometimes wait for us, and it is possible to become deeply aware of its waiting. The quality of time alters then, like a change in the light, because the present is so thoroughly shadowed by other seasons: the revived or receding past, the newly unmeasurable future, the unimaginable time beyond time. With such moments we arrive at the conditions for the special sense of lateness that is the subject of this book.

It's worth pausing over the delicately shifting meanings of the word *late*, ranging from missed appointments through the cycles of nature to vanished life. Most frequently perhaps *late* just means "too late," later than we should be, not on time. But late evenings, late blossoms, and late autumns are perfectly punctual—there isn't another clock or calendar they are supposed to match. Dead persons have certainly got themselves beyond time, but then what difficult temporal longing lurks in our calling them "late"? Lateness doesn't name a single relation to time, but it always brings time in its wake. It is a way of remembering time, whether it is missed or met or gone.

"Conversion of time into space," Edward Said wrote in one of his notes for a famous course he taught at Columbia, "Last Works/Late Style." "Opening up of chronological sequence into landscape the better to be able to *see, experience, grasp* and *work* with time. . . . Adorno: fractured landscape as objective" (Said's italics). The note goes on to mention several passages in Proust and three poems by Hopkins. All of the Proust passages come from the end of *In Search of Lost Time,* where the narrator is simultaneously enchanted by his new insights into the recoverability of the past and anguished at the shortness of the years or months that are probably left to him. He sees a person as a crossroads, time as a body, "characters as duration," as Said's note says. With Hopkins, Said is thinking of the darkening landscapes the poet so loves, of the "winter world" that "yields . . . with some sighs, our explanation,"[2] and above all, perhaps, of a terrifying picture of sleep and death as our only escape from the steep drops and fierce weather of the mind:

> *O the mind, mind has mountains; cliffs of fall*
> *Frightful, sheer, no-man-fathomed. Hold them cheap*
> *May who ne'er hung there. Nor does long our small*
> *Durance deal with that steep or deep. Here! creep,*
> *Wretch, under a comfort serves in a whirlwind: all*
> *Life death does end and each day dies with sleep.*[3]

These are examples of (I quote from the course description for "Last Works/Late Style") "artists . . . whose work expresses lateness through the peculiarities of its style," and clearly those "peculiarities" go beyond converting time into space. Adorno's "fractured landscape" is only one of the ways in which late works quarrel with time and manage to represent death, as he puts it, "in a refracted mode, as allegory." This angle of refraction is important for Said, too. "Late style"—the term is Adorno's—can't be a direct result of aging or death, because style is not a mortal creature, and works of art have no organic life to lose. But the approaching death of the artist gets into the works all the same, and in many different ways; the privileged forms, as Said wrote, are "anachronism and anomaly." He had a canon of such artists, including those already quoted, and almost all of them appear in some form in this book: Adorno himself, Thomas Mann, Richard Strauss, Jean Genet, Giuseppe Tomasi di Lampedusa, C. P. Cavafy. There are others, too, who appear in separate articles Said published toward the end of his life: Euripides, Britten, even—in one opera at least—Mozart, where a sudden lateness, as distinct from maturity, produces, as we read in this book, "a special ironic expressiveness well beyond the words and the situation."

This type of lateness is quite different, Said argued, from the unearthly serenity we find in the last works of Sophocles and Shakespeare. *Oedipus at Colonus, The Tempest,* and *The Winter's Tale* are late enough in their way, but they have settled their quarrel with time. "Each of us," Said writes in the first chapter of this book, "can readily supply evidence of how it is that late works crown a lifetime of aesthetic endeavor. Rembrandt and Matisse, Bach and Wagner. But what of artistic lateness not as harmony and resolution, but as intransigence, difficulty and unresolved contradiction?" And what of an artist like Glenn Gould, who created his own form of lateness by removing himself from the world of live performance, intransigently becoming posthumous, so to speak, while still intensely active?

Said owes a great debt to Adorno, which he repeatedly acknowledges. He was "the only true follower of Adorno," he said in a late interview. (This was the same interview, with *Ha'aretz Magazine,* Tel Aviv, in which he said he was "the last

Jewish intellectual.")⁴ He was joking, but the joke was about the idea of Adorno having followers (or Said's following him all that closely) and not about the importance of the example. Still, Said differed from the melancholy master in crucial ways. He didn't think his own kind of lateness was the only kind that mattered, and he thought Adorno missed "the tragic dimension" of all this difficulty.⁵ He also thought that Adorno's "totally administered society," while always a threat, was not everywhere a reality. "Pleasure and privacy do remain," Said wrote in *Musical Elaborations,* and in a memorable phrase, thinking of Brahms, he evoked "the music of his music"—the intimate music that lingers when every allowance has been made for the politics and economics of any worldly art.⁶

Lateness for Said is "a form of exile," as he says in this book, but even exiles live somewhere, and "late style is *in,* but oddly *apart* from, the present." "For Adorno," Said comments, "lateness is the idea of surviving beyond what is acceptable and normal; in addition, lateness includes the idea that one cannot really go beyond lateness at all." This is precisely what keeps us in time even when we seem to be out of time, and lateness has its playful as well as its tragic aspects. The late style of Richard Strauss, for example, as seen and heard in *Der Rosenkavalier* and *Ariadne auf Naxos,* is certainly "unsettling," but only because it so resolutely substitutes another time for the brutal present. "Truly this world is pre-historical in its freedom from daily pressures and cares, and in its seemingly limitless capacity for self-indulgence, amusement, and luxury: and this too is a characteristic of twentieth-century late style."

It is part of the generosity of Said's critical imagination that he sees "amusement" as a form of resistance. He can do this because amusement, like pleasure and privacy, does not require reconciliation with a status quo or a dominant regime, and it is this version of freedom that unites all the instances of lateness in this book. The tone of the individual cases may be tragic, comic, ironic, parodic, and much else, but every artist who is late in Said's sense of the word will be unreconciled. Adorno writes of Beethoven's refusal to "reconcile into a single image what is not reconciled,"[7] and this is the note we hear again and again in Said's remarks about music and about the world. "What I find valuable in Adorno is this notion of tension, of highlighting and dramatizing what I call irreconcilabilities (ESR 437)." He calls irreconcilabilities what other people call road maps, but unlike Adorno he doesn't despair, and he doesn't accept cultural or political standoffs. It's true that dreams of reconciliation, in music or in the Middle East, are often merely a means of failing to think about difficulty and difference. But that doesn't mean such thinking isn't possible, and reconciliation may in any case not be exactly what we need. Said insisted, as Stathis Gourgouris reminds us in a recent essay, that "all criticism is postulated and performed on the assumption that it is to have a future." "Late style," Gourgouris continues, "is precisely the form that defies the infirmities of the present, as well as the palliatives of the past, in order to seek out this future, to posit it and perform it even if in words and images, gestures and representations, that now seem puzzling, untimely, or impossible."[8]

There are hints of ideas about late style, and a citation of Adorno's 1938 essay on Beethoven, in *Musical Elaborations*, given as the Wellek Lectures at Irvine in 1989 and published in 1990, and Said seems to have begun work on his Columbia course sometime after that. When he gave the three Lord Northcliffe Lectures in London in 1993, certain key ideas and examples were well developed, and these lectures now form the basis of chapters 1, 2, and 5 of this book. In the meantime two things had happened. Said's mother had died before the publication of *Musical Elaborations*. He tells us in that book that they "shared many musical experiences together," and adds, "I am more sorry than I can say that, regardless of its flaws, she did not live to read this book and tell me what she thought. (ME xi)." To anyone who knows the family, these words have a special poignancy, since Mrs. Said was a very articulate woman of very firm mind. In my memory, whenever she came to stay in New York—we lived in the same building for a long time— mother and son, both early risers, always seemed to have had several lively arguments before anyone else got up. And then in September 1991, as a result of an ordinary medical checkup, Said discovered that he had leukemia. These two events, as he said several times, led him to the writing of his memoir *Out of Place*, started in 1994 and published in 1999. "I don't think that I was ever consciously afraid of dying," he said, "though I soon grew aware of the shortage of time (ESR 419)."

He had plenty to do: teaching, traveling, lecturing, working on the memoir, and doing all the writing collected in the later pages of *Reflections on Exile* (1998), in *The End of the Peace Process* (2000), in *Power, Politics, and Culture* (2001), in *Parallels and Paradoxes* (2002), in *Humanism and Democratic Criticism* (2004), and in *From Oslo to Iraq and the Road Map* (2004). He also seemed to be on the telephone all the time, and I sometimes thought of him as a version of the writer in Henry James's story "The Private Life," who spends so much of his life in society that he can't possibly be producing the books he is manifestly producing. So the edging out of the projected book on late style, which Said often spoke of, doesn't really need an explanation.

And yet I find I can't believe that he wanted to finish this book. Or rather, he wanted to finish it but was waiting for a time that would perhaps never have come. There would have been a time for this book about untimeliness, but this time was always: not quite yet. Completing the work would have been too much like writing the end of a life, closing the long chapter about the making of the self that opened with Said's book *Beginnings* or, even earlier, with his book on Conrad—and the whole point about beginnings, as distinct from origins, is that they are chosen. I keep thinking of Said's evocation of Richard Strauss's late work as "radically, beautifully elaborative," as "music whose pleasures and discoveries are premised upon letting go (ME 105)." These words were written well before the diagnosis of September 1991, but then Said's interest in late style or anything else was never merely autobiographical. Thoughts of his own death deepened his attachment to the question of late style; they didn't instigate it. But I do believe these thoughts became part of the projected book's long and incomplete life. It's one thing to write of letting go, and another to do it. Explorations of the making of the self can go until the very end; the self's unmaking is another affair, and late style comes close to that.

Is this to say that Said himself didn't have a late style? He certainly had the politics and the morality he associated with late style, a devotion to the truth of unreconciled relations, and in this sense his own work joins the company of the essays, poems, novels, films, and operas he writes about. But lateness is not all, any more than ripeness is, and Said found the same politics and morality, the same passions, in other places and persons; indeed they are his own earlier politics and morality and passions. Lateness "elucidates and dramatizes (ME 21)," as he says in another context, makes it hard for us to go on with our delusions. We can do this without any thought of death, and Said specifically identified this task as that of the intellectual—in this perspective Glenn Gould, seeking to question and remake the relation of music to the social world of performance, is Said's model of the intellectual. My sense is that for all his deep interest in lateness and his awareness of the shortage of his own time, Said was not attracted by the idea of a late, dissolving self. He doesn't inhabit his last works as "a lamenting personality," his own phrase in this book for Adorno's picture of late Beethoven. Said wanted to continue with the self's making, and if we divide a life into early, middle, and late periods, he was still in the middle when he died at the age of sixty-seven in September 2003, twelve years after the first diagnosis of leukemia. Still a little too early, I think he would have said, for real lateness.

The book on late style was unfinished, then, but the materials for it are very rich. We can regret what might have been and do our saddened best to imagine what Said might have written if he had written more, but we have no reason to be ungrateful for what there is. In what follows I have put together several different sets of materials, but although I have cut and spliced, I have not thought it necessary to write summaries or bridging passages. The words are all Said's own. The Lord Northcliffe Lectures, as I mentioned earlier, form the basis of chapters 1, 2, and 5 of this book, with an overview taken from an article called "Late Style" that appeared in the *London Review of Books*. This article included some thoughts on Cavafy and dropped all the earlier writing on Visconti's film *The Leopard,* as well as a good deal of the Adorno material. This work is now restored to the relevant places. In the first chapter I have also used the introduction of a talk Said gave in December 2000 to a group of doctors (including his own physician) in New York. Chapters 3, 4, and 6, on Mozart, Genet, and Gould respectively, were written as individual essays. Chapter 7 is my assemblage of four different elements: some remarks taken from a review of Maynard Solomon's book on Beethoven; an essay on productions of Euripides; the Cavafy material from the *London Review* article; and an essay on Britten's *Death in Venice*.

This sequence brings us back to Adorno and the idea of the catastrophic work of art, and that seems an appropriate place to stop. But stopping is not ending, and we should remember this here not only because Said didn't complete this book himself but because style for him was also a question of what style couldn't say. "I've always been interested in what gets left out," he said in an interview. "I'm interested in the tension between what is represented and what isn't represented, between the articulate and the silent (ESR 424)." In such a view silence itself is an aspect of style, "not as simple as saying nothing," as Said remarks in an unpublished note. "We are a people of message and signals," he says of the Palestinians, "of allusions and indirect expression."[9] What he calls the "reticence" of music, its "allusive silence (ME 16)," offers us its deepest pleasures and also a hint of hope amid political and other hopelessness, a sense of "that precarious exilic realm" where we "first truly grasp the difficulty of what cannot be grasped and then go forth to try anyway."[10]

Michael Wood
Princeton, New Jersey,
April 2005

ON
LATE
STYLE

ONE

Timeliness and Lateness

The relationship between bodily condition and aesthetic style seems at first to be a subject so irrelevant and perhaps even trivial by comparison with the momentousness of life, mortality, medical science, and health, as to be quickly dismissed. Nevertheless, my contention is as follows: all of us, by virtue of the simple fact of being conscious, are involved in constantly thinking about and making something of our lives, self-making being one of the bases of history, which according to Ibn Khaldun and Vico, the great founders of the science of history, is essentially the product of human labor.

The important distinction therefore is that between the realm of nature on the one hand and secular human history on the other. The body, its health, its care, composition, functioning, and flourishing, its illnesses and demise, belong to the order of nature; what we *understand* of that nature, however, how we see and live it in our consciousness, how we create a sense of our life individually and collectively, subjectively as well as socially, how we divide it into periods, belongs roughly speaking to the order of history that when we reflect on it we can recall, analyze, and meditate on, constantly changing its shape in the process. There are all sorts of connections between the two realms, between history and nature, but for now I want to keep them apart and focus only on one of them, history.

Being myself a profoundly secular person, I have for years been studying this self-making process through three great problematics, three great human episodes common to all cultures and traditions, and it is the third of these problematics that I want specifically to discuss in this book. But for purposes of clarity, let me quickly summarize one and two. The first is the whole notion of beginning, the moment of birth and origin, which in the context of history is all the material that goes into thinking about how a given process, its establishment and institution, life, project, and so on, gets started. Thirty years ago I published a book called *Beginnings: Intention and Method* about how the mind finds it necessary at certain times to retrospectively locate a point of origin for itself as to how things begin in the most elementary sense with birth. In fields like history and the study of culture, memory and retrospection draw us to the onset of important things—for example, the beginnings of industrialization, of scientific medicine, of the romantic period, and so on. Individually, the chronology of discovery is as important for a scientist as it is for someone like Immanuel Kant who reads David Hume for the first time and, he says memorably, is briskly awakened from his dogmatic slumber. In Western literature, the form of the novel is coincidental with the emergence of the bourgeoisie in the late seventeenth century, and this is why, for its first century, the novel is all about birth, possible orphanhood, the discovery of roots, and the creation of a new world, a career, and society. *Robinson Crusoe. Tom Jones. Tristram Shandy.*

To locate a beginning in retrospective time is to ground a project (such as an experiment, or a governmental commission, or Dickens's beginning to write *Bleak House*) in that moment, which is always subject to revision. Beginnings of this sort necessarily involve an intention that either is fulfilled, totally or in part, or is viewed as totally failed, in successive time. And so the second great problematic is about the continuity that occurs after birth, the exfoliation from a beginning: in the time from birth to youth, reproductive generation, maturity. Every culture offers and circulates images of what has been wonderfully called the dialectic of incarnation, or in François Jacob's phrase, *la logique du vivant*. Again to give examples from the history of the novel (the Western aesthetic form that offers the largest and most complex image of ourselves that we have), there is the bildungsroman or novel of education, the novel of idealism and disappointment *(education sentimentale, illusions perdues)*, the novel of immaturity and community (like George Eliot's *Middlemarch,* which the English critic Gillian Beer has shown was powerfully influenced by what she calls Darwin's plots for the patterns of generation that structure this great novel of nineteenth-century British society). Other aesthetic forms, in music and painting, follow similar patterns.

But there are also exceptions, examples of deviation from the overall assumed pattern to human life. One thinks of *Gulliver's Travels, Crime and Punishment,* and *The Trial,* works that seem to break away from the amazingly persistent underlying compact between the notion of the successive ages of man (as in Shakespeare) and aesthetic reflections of and on them. For it bears saying explicitly that both in art and in our general ideas about the passage of human life there is assumed to be a general abiding *timeliness,* by which I mean that what is appropriate to early life is not appropriate for later stages, and vice versa. You will recall, for example, the stern biblical observation that to everything there is a season and a time, to every purpose under the heaven, a time to be born, and a time to die, and so on: "wherefore I perceive that there is nothing better, than that a man should rejoice in his own works; for that is his portion: for who shall bring him to see what shall be after him? . . . All things come alike to all: there is one event to the righteous, and to the wicked; to the good and to the clean, and to the unclean."

In other words, we assume that the essential health of a human life has a great deal to do with its correspondence to its time, the fitting together of one to the other, and therefore its appropriateness or timeliness. Comedy, for instance, seeks its material in untimely behavior, an old man falling in love with a young woman (May in December), as in Molière and Chaucer, a philosopher acting like a child, a well person feigning illness. But it is also comedy as a form that brings about the restoration of timeliness through the *kommos* with which the work usually concludes, the marriage of young lovers.

I come finally to the last great problematic, which for obvious personal reasons is my subject here—the last or late period of life, the decay of the body, the onset of ill health or other factors that even in a younger person bring on the possibility of an untimely end. I shall focus on great artists and how near the end of their lives their work and thought acquires a new idiom, what I shall be calling a late style.

Does one grow wiser with age, and are there unique qualities of perception and form that artists acquire as a result of age in the late phase of their career? We meet the accepted notion of age and wisdom in some last works that reflect a special maturity, a new spirit of reconciliation and serenity often expressed in terms of a miraculous transfiguration of common reality. In late plays such as *The Tempest* or *The Winter's Tale*, Shakespeare returns to the forms of romance and parable; similarly, in Sophocles' *Oedipus at Colonus*, the aged hero is portrayed as having finally attained a remarkable holiness and sense of resolution. Or there is the well-known case of Verdi who, in his final years, produced *Othello* and *Falstaff*, works that exude not so much a spirit of wise resignation as a renewed, almost youthful energy that attests to an apotheosis of artistic creativity and power.

Each of us can readily supply evidence of how it is that late works crown a lifetime of aesthetic endeavor. Rembrandt and Matisse, Bach and Wagner. But what of artistic lateness not as harmony and resolution but as intransigence, difficulty, and unresolved contradiction? What if age and ill health don't produce the serenity of "ripeness is all"? This is the case with Ibsen, whose final works, especially *When We Dead Awaken,* tear apart the career and the artist's craft and reopen the questions of meaning, success, and progress that the artist's late period is supposed to move beyond. Far from resolution, then, Ibsen's last plays suggest an angry and disturbed artist for whom the medium of drama provides an occasion to stir up more anxiety, tamper irrevocably with the possibility of closure, and leave the audience more perplexed and unsettled than before.

It is this second type of lateness as a factor of style that I find deeply interesting. I'd like to explore the experience of late style that involves a nonharmonious, nonserene tension, and above all, a sort of deliberately unproductive productiveness going *against.* . . .

Adorno used the phrase "late style" most memorably in an essay fragment entitled "Spätstil Beethovens," dated 1937 and included in a 1964 collection of musical essays, *Moments musicaux,* then again in *Essays on Music,* a posthumously published (1993) book on Beethoven.[1] For Adorno, far more than for anyone who has spoken of Beethoven's last works, those compositions that belong to what is known as the composer's third period (the last five piano sonatas, the Ninth Symphony, the *Missa Solemnis,* the last six string quartets, the seventeen bagatelles for piano) constitute an event in the history of modern culture: a moment when the artist who is fully in command of his medium nevertheless abandons communication with the established social order of which he is a part and achieves a contradictory, alienated relationship with it. His late works constitute a form of exile. One of Adorno's most extraordinary essays, included in the same collection with the late-style fragment, is on the *Missa Solemnis,* which he calls an alienated masterpiece *(verfremdetes Hauptwerk)* by virtue of its difficulty, its archaisms, and its strange subjective revaluation of the Mass (EM 569–83).

What Adorno had to say about late Beethoven throughout his voluminous writings (Adorno died in 1969) is clearly a philosophical construction that served as a sort of beginning point for all his analyses of subsequent music. So convincing as cultural symbol to Adorno was the figure of the aging, deaf, and isolated composer that it even turned up as part of Adorno's contribution to Thomas Mann's *Doktor Faustus,* in which young Adrian Leverkühn is impressed by a lecture on Beethoven's final period given by Wendell Kretschmar, and you can perceive in the following passage how unhealthy it all seems:

> Beethoven's art had overgrown itself, risen out of the habitable regions of tradition, even before the startled gaze of human eyes, into spheres of the entirely and utterly and nothing—but personal—an ego painfully isolated in the absolute, isolated too from sense by the loss of his hearing; lonely prince of a realm of spirits, from whom now only a chilling breath issued to terrify his most willing contemporaries, standing as they did aghast at these communications of which only at moments, only by exception, they could understand anything at all.[2]

This is almost pure Adorno. There is heroism in it but also intransigence. Nothing about the essence of the late Beethoven is reducible to the notion of art as a document—that is, to a reading of the music that stresses "reality breaking through" in the form of history or the composer's sense of his impending death. For "in this way," if one stresses the works only as an expression of Beethoven's personality, Adorno says, "the late works are relegated to the outer reaches of art, in the vicinity of document. In fact, studies of the very late Beethoven seldom fail to make reference to biography and fate. It is as if, confronted by the dignity of human death, the theory of art were to divest itself of its rights and abdicate in favor of reality" (EM 564). Late style is what happens if art does not abdicate its rights in favor of reality.

Impending death is there, of course, and cannot be denied. But Adorno's stress is on the formal law of Beethoven's final compositional mode, by which he means the rights of the aesthetic. This law reveals itself to be a peculiar amalgam of subjectivity and convention, evident in such devices as "decorative trill sequences, cadences and fiorituras" (EM 565). In a formulation of what that subjectivity is, Adorno says:

This law is revealed precisely in the thought of death. . . . Death is imposed only on created beings, not on works of art, and thus it has appeared in art only in a refracted mode, as allegory. . . . The power of subjectivity in the late works of art is the irascible gesture with which it takes leave of the works themselves. It breaks their bonds, not in order to express itself, but in order, expressionless, to cast off the appearance of art. Of the works themselves it leaves only fragments behind, and communicates itself, like a cipher, only through the blank spaces from which it has disengaged itself. Touched

by death, the hand of the master sets free the masses of material that he used to form; its tears and fissures, witnesses to the
finite powerlessness of the I confronted with Being, are its
final work [*der endlichen Ohnmacht des Ichs vorm Seienden,
sind ihr letztes Werk*]. (EM 566)

What has evidently gripped Adorno in Beethoven's late work is
its episodic character, its apparent disregard for its own continuity. If we compare a middle-period work, such as the *Eroica*
with the opus 110 sonata, we will be struck with the totally
cogent and integrative driven logic of the former and the somewhat distracted, often extremely careless and repetitive character of the latter. The opening theme in the thirty-first sonata
is spaced very awkwardly, and when it moves on after the trill,
its accompaniment—a studentlike, almost clumsy repetitive
figure—is, Adorno correctly says, "unabashedly primitive."
And so it goes in the late works, massive polyphonic writing
of the most abstruse and difficult sort alternating with what
Adorno calls "conventions" that are often seemingly unmoti-
vated rhetorical devices like trills, or appogiaturas whose role
in the work seems unintegrated into the structure. Adorno says:
"His late work still remains process, but not as development;
rather as a catching fire between extremes, which no longer
allow for any secure middle ground or harmony of spontane-
ity." Thus, as Kretschmar says in Mann's *Doktor Faustus,*
Beethoven's late works often communicate an impression
of being unfinished—something that the energetic teacher of
Adrian Leverkühn discusses at great and ingenious length in
his disquisition about the two movements of opus 111.

Adorno's thesis is that all this is predicated upon two considerations: first, that when he was a young composer, Beethoven's
work was vigorous and organically whole, whereas it has now
become more wayward and eccentric; and second, that as an

older man facing death, Beethoven realizes that his work pro-
claims, as Rose Subotnik puts it, that "no synthesis is conceiv-
able [but is in effect] the remains of a synthesis, the vestige of
an individual human subject sorely aware of the wholeness,
and consequently the survival, that has eluded it forever."[3]
Beethoven's late works therefore communicate a tragic sense in
spite of their irascibility. How exactly and poignantly Adorno
discovers this is readily evident at the end of his essay on
Beethoven's late style. Noting that in Beethoven, as in Goethe,
there is a plethora of "unmastered material," he goes on to
observe that in the late sonatas conventions, for instance, are
"splintered off" from the main thrust of the compositions,
"fallen away and abandoned." As for the great *unisons* (in the
Ninth Symphony or the *Missa*), they stand next to huge polyphonic ensembles. Adorno then adds:

> It is subjectivity that forcibly brings the extremes together
> in the moment, fills the dense polyphony with its tensions,
> breaks it apart with the *unisono*, and disengages itself, leav-
> ing the naked tone behind; that sets the mere phrase as a
> monument to what has been, marking a subjectivity turned
> to stone. The cesuras, the sudden discontinuities that more
> than anything else characterize the very late Beethoven, are
> those moments of breaking away; the work is silent at the
> instant when it is left behind, and turns its emptiness outward.
> (EM 567)

What Adorno describes here is the way Beethoven seems to
inhabit the late works as a lamenting personality, then seems
to leave the work or phrases in it incomplete, abruptly dropped,
as in the opening of the F Major Quartet or the A Minor. The
sense of abandonment is peculiarly acute in comparison with
the driven and relentless quality of second-period works such

as the Fifth Symphony, where, at moments like the ending of
the fourth movement, Beethoven cannot seem to tear himself
away from the piece. Thus, to conclude, Adorno says that the
style of the late works is both objective and subjective:

> Objective is the fractured landscape, subjective the light in
> which—alone—it glows into life. He does not bring about
> their harmonious synthesis. As the power of dissociation, he
> tears them apart in time, in order perhaps, to preserve them
> for the eternal. In the history of art, late works are the catas-
> trophes. (EM 567)

The crux, as always in Adorno, is the problem of trying to
say what holds the works together, gives them unity, makes
them more than just a collection of fragments. Here he is at his
most paradoxical: one cannot say what connects the parts
other than by invoking "the figure they create together." Neither can one minimize the differences among the parts, and it
would appear that actually *naming* the unity, or giving it a specific identity, would then reduce its catastrophic force. Thus the
power of Beethoven's late style is negative, or rather *it is nega-
tivity*: where one would expect serenity and maturity, one
instead finds a bristling, difficult, and unyielding—perhaps
even inhuman—challenge. "The maturity of the late works,"
Adorno says, "does not resemble the kind one finds in fruit.
They are . . . not round, but furrowed, even ravaged. Devoid of
sweetness, bitter and spiny, they do not surrender themselves to
mere delectation" (EM 564). Beethoven's late works remain
unreconciled, uncoopted by a higher synthesis: they do not fit
any scheme, and they cannot be reconciled or resolved, since
their irresolution and unsynthesized fragmentariness are constitutive, neither ornamental nor symbolic of something else.

Beethoven's late compositions are in fact about "lost totality," and are therefore catastrophic.

Here we must return to the notion of lateness. Late in what sense? For Adorno, *lateness* is the idea of surviving beyond what is acceptable and normal; in addition, lateness includes the idea that one cannot really go beyond lateness at all, cannot transcend or lift oneself out of lateness, but can only deepen the lateness. There is no transcendence or unity. In his book *The Philosophy of New Music,* Adorno says Schoenberg essentially prolonged the irreconcilabilities, negations, and immobilities of the late Beethoven. And of course, lateness retains in it the late phase of a human life.

Two further points. The reason Beethoven's late style so gripped Adorno throughout his writing is that in a completely paradoxical way, Beethoven's immobilized and socially resistant final works are at the core of what is new in modern music of our own time. In Beethoven's middle-period opera *Fidelio*— the quintessential middle-period work—the idea of humanity is manifest throughout, and with it an idea of a better world. Similarly for Hegel, irreconcilable opposites were resolvable by means of the dialectic, with a reconciliation of opposites, a *grand* synthesis, at the end. Late-style Beethoven keeps the irreconcilable apart, and in so doing "music is transformed more and more from something significant into something obscure—even to itself."[4] Thus late-style Beethoven presides over music's rejection of the new bourgeois order and forecasts the totally authentic and *novel* art of Schoenberg, whose "advanced music has no recourse but to insist on its own ossification without concession to that would-be humanitarianism which it sees through. . . . Under the present circumstances [music] is restricted to definitive negation" (PNM 20). Second, far from being simply an eccentric and irrelevant phenomenon, late-style Beethoven, remorselessly alienated and obscure, becomes the prototypical modern aesthetic form, and by virtue of its distance from and rejection of bourgeois society and even a quiet death, it acquires an even greater significance and defiance for that very reason.

And in so many ways, the concept of lateness, as well as what goes with it in these astonishingly bold and bleak ruminations on the position of an aging artist, comes for Adorno to seem *the* fundamental aspect of aesthetics and of his own work as critical theorist and philosopher. My reading of Adorno, with his reflections about music at its center, sees him as injecting Marxism with a vaccine so powerful as to dissolve its agitational force almost completely. Not only do the notions of advance and culmination in Marxism crumble under his rigorous negative scorn, but so too does anything that suggests movement at all. With death and senescence before him, with a promising start years behind him, Adorno uses the model of late Beethoven to endure ending in the form of *lateness* but *for itself,* its own sake, not as a preparation for or obliteration of something else. Lateness is being at the end, fully conscious, full of memory, and also very (even preternaturally) aware of the present. Adorno, like Beethoven, becomes therefore a figure of lateness itself, an untimely, scandalous, even catastrophic commentator on the present.

No one needs to be reminded that Adorno is exceptionally difficult to read, whether in his original German or in any number of translations. Fredric Jameson speaks very well about the sheer intelligence of his sentences, their incomparable refinement, their programmatically complex internal movement, their way of almost routinely foiling a first or second or third attempt at paraphrasing their content. Adorno's prose style violates various norms: he assumes little community of understanding between himself and his audience; he is slow, unjournalistic, unpackageable, unskimmable. Even an auto-biographical text like *Minima Moralia* is an assault on biographical, narrative, or anecdotal continuity; its form exactly replicates its subtitle—reflections from damaged life—a cascading series of discontinuous fragments, all of them in some way assaulting suspicious "wholes," fictitious unities presided over by Hegel, whose grand synthesis has derisive contempt for the individual. "The conception of a totality through all its antagonisms compels him [Hegel] to assign to individualism, however much he may designate it a driving moment in the process, an inferior status in the construction of the whole."[5]

Adorno's counter to false, and in Hegel's case untenable, totalities is not just to say that they are inauthentic but in fact to write, to *be,* an alternative through exile and subjectivity, albeit exile and subjectivity addressed to philosophic issues. Moreover he says, "Social analysis can learn incomparably more from individual experience than Hegel conceded, while conversely the large historical categories . . . are no longer above suspicion of fraud" (MM 17). In the performance of unreconciled individual critical thinking there is "the force of protest." Yes, such critical thought as Adorno's is very idiosyncratic and often very obscure but, as he wrote in "Resignation," his last essay, "the uncompromisingly critical thinker, who neither superscribes his conscience nor permits himself to be terrorized into action, is in truth the one who does not give in." To work through the silences and fissures is to avoid packaging and administration and is in fact to accept and perform the *lateness* of his position. "Whatever has once been thought can be suppressed, forgotten, can even vanish. For thinking has the momentum of the general. [Here Adorno means both that individual thought is part of the general culture of the age and that, because it is individual, it generates its own momentum yet veers or swerves off from the general.] What once was

thought cogently must be thought elsewhere, by others: this
confidence accompanies even the most solitary and powerless
thought."[6]

Lateness therefore is a kind of self-imposed exile from what
is generally acceptable, coming after it, and surviving beyond
it. Hence Adorno's evaluation of the late Beethoven and his
own lesson for his reader. The catastrophe represented by
late style for Adorno is that in Beethoven's case the music
is episodic, fragmentary, riven with the absences and silences
that can neither be filled by supplying some general scheme
for them, nor be ignored and diminished by saying "poor
Beethoven, he was deaf, he was approaching death, these are
lapses we shall overlook."

Years after the first Beethoven essay appeared and in a
sort of counterblast to his book on new music Adorno published an essay called "Das Ältern der neuen Musik," the aging
of the new music. He spoke there of advanced music that had
inherited the discoveries of the second Viennese School and had
gone on "to show symptoms of false satisfaction" by becoming collectivized, affirmative, safe. New music was negative,
"the result of something distressing and confused" (EM 181).
Adorno recalls how traumatic to their audiences were the
first performances of Berg's *Altenberg Songs* and Stravinsky's
The Rite of Spring. That was the true force of new music, fearlessly drawing out the consequences of Beethoven's late-style
compositions. Today, however, so-called new music has simply
aged beyond Beethoven. "More than a hundred years ago
Kierkegaard, speaking as a theologian, said that where once a
dreadful abyss yawned a railroad bridge now stretches, from
which the passengers can look comfortably down into the
depths. The situation of [aged modern] music is no different"
(EM 183).

Just as the negative power of late Beethoven derives from

its dissonant relationship with the affirmative developmental thrust of his second-period music, so too the dissonances of Webern and Schoenberg occur "surrounded by a shudder"; "they are felt as something uncanny and are introduced by their authors with fear and trembling" (EM 185). To reproduce the dissonances academically or institutionally a generation later without risk or stakes either emotionally or in actuality, says Adorno, is completely to lose the shattering force of the new. If you just line up a bunch of tone rows happily, or if you hold festivals of advanced music, you lose the core of, for instance, Webern's achievement, which was to juxtapose "twelve tone technique . . . [with] its antithesis, the explosive power of the musically individual"; now an aging as opposed to a late art, modern music amounts to little more than "an empty, high-spirited trip, through thinkably complex scores, in which nothing actually occurs" (EM 185, 187).

There is therefore an inherent tension in late style that abjures mere bourgeois aging and that insists on the increasing sense of apartness and exile and anachronism, which late style expresses and, more important, uses to formally sustain itself. One has the impression reading Adorno, from the aphoristic essays on such things as punctuation marks and book covers collected in *Noten zur Literatur* to the grand theoretical works like *Negative Dialectics* and *Aesthetic Theory,* that what he looked for in style was the evidence he found in late Beethoven of sustained tension, unaccommodated stubbornness, lateness and newness next to each other by virtue of an "inexorable clamp that holds together what no less powerfully strives to break apart" (EM 186). Above all, late style as exemplified by Beethoven and Schoenberg cannot be replicated by invitation, or by lazy reproduction, or by mere dynastic or narrative reproduction. There is a paradox: how essentially unrepeatable, uniquely articulated aesthetic works written not at the beginning but at the end of a career can nevertheless have an influence on what comes after them. And how does that influence enter and inform the work of the critic, whose whole enterprise stubbornly prizes its own intransigence and untimeliness?

Philosophically Adorno is unthinkable without the majestic beacon provided by Lukács's *History and Class Consciousness,* but he is also unthinkable without his refusal of the earlier work's triumphalism and implied transcendence. If for Lukács the subject-object relationship and its antinomies, the fragmentation and the lostness, the ironic perspectivism of modernity, were supremely discerned, embodied, and consummated in narrative forms such as the rewritten epics both of the novel and the proletariat's class consciousness, for Adorno that particular choice was, he said in a famous anti-Lukács essay, a kind of false reconciliation under duress. Modernity was a fallen, unredeemed reality, and new music, as much as Adorno's own philosophic practice, took its task to be a ceaselessly demonstrated reminder of that reality.

Were this reminder to be simply a repeated *no* or *this will not do,* late style and philosophy would be totally uninteresting and repetitive. There must be a *constructive* element above all, which animates the procedure. What Adorno finds so admirable about Schoenberg is his severity as well as his invention of a technique that provides music with an alternative to tonal harmony and to classical inflection, color, rhythm. Adorno describes the twelve-tone method of Schoenberg in terms taken almost verbatim from Lukács's drama of the subject-object impasse, but each time there is an opportunity for synthesis, Adorno has Schoenberg turn it down. What we see is Adorno constructing a breathtakingly regressive sequence, an endgame procedure by which he threads his way back along the route taken by Lukács; all the laboriously devised solutions volunteered by Lukács for pulling himself out of the slough of modern despair are just as laboriously dismantled and rendered useless by Adorno's account of what Schoenberg was really about. Fixated on the new music's absolute rejection of the commercial sphere, Adorno's words cut out the social ground from underneath art. For in fighting ornament, illusion, reconciliation, communication, humanism, and success, art becomes untenable.

> Everything having no function in the work of art—and therefore everything transcending the law of mere existence—is withdrawn. The function of the work of art lies precisely in its transcendence beyond mere existence. . . . Since the work of art, after all, cannot be reality, the elimination of all illusory features accentuates all the more glaringly the illusory character of its existence. This process is inescapable. (PNM 70)

Are late-style Beethoven and Schoenberg actually like this, we finally ask, and is their music so isolated in its antithesis to society? Or is it the case that Adorno's descriptions of them are models, paradigms, constructs intended to highlight certain features and thereby give the two composers a certain appearance, a certain profile in and for Adorno's own writing? What Adorno does is theoretical—that is, his construction isn't supposed to be a replica of the real thing, which had he attempted it would have been little more than a packaged and domesticated copy. The location of Adorno's writing is theory, a space where he can construct his demystifying negative dialectics. Whether he writes about music or literature or abstract philosophy or society, Adorno's theoretical work is always in a strange way extremely concrete—that is, he writes from the perspective of long experience rather than revolutionary beginnings, and what he writes about is saturated in culture. Adorno's position as a theorist of late style and of endgames is an extraordinary *knowingness,* the polar opposite of Rousseau's. There is also the supposition (indeed the assumption) of wealth and privilege, what today we call elitism and, more recently, political incorrectness. Adorno's world is the world of Weimar, of high modernism, of luxury tastes, of an inspired if slightly sated amateurism. Never was he more autobiographical than in the first fragment, entitled "For Marcel Proust," of *Minima Moralia:*

> The son of well-to-do parents, who whether from talent or weakness, engages in a so-called intellectual profession, as an artist or a scholar, will have a particularly difficult time with those bearing the distasteful title of colleagues. It is not merely that his independence is envied, the seriousness of his intentions mistrusted, and that he is suspected of being a secret envoy of the established powers. *Such suspicions,* though betraying a secret resentment, *would usually prove well-founded.* But the real resistances lie elsewhere. The occupation with things of the mind has by now itself become "practical," a business with strict division of labor, departments and restricted entry. The man of independent means who chooses it out of repugnance for the ignominy of earning money will not be disposed to acknowledge the fact. For this he is punished. He is not a "professional," is ranked in the competitive hierarchy as a dilettante no matter how well he knows his subject, and must, if he wants a career, show himself even more resolutely blinkered than the most inveterate specialist. (MM 21; emphases added)

The dynastic fact of importance here is that his parents were wealthy. No less important is the sentence where, having described his colleagues as being envious as well as suspicious of his relationship with "the established powers," Adorno adds that these suspicions are well founded. Which is to say that in a contest between the blandishments of an intellectual Faubourg St. Honoré and those afforded by the moral equivalent of a working-class association, Adorno would end up with the former, not the latter. On one level his elitist predilections are of course a function of his class background. But on another what he likes in it, well after his defection from its ranks, is its sense of ease and luxury; this, he implies in *Minima Moralia*, allows him a continuous familiarity with great works, great masters, and great ideas, not as subjects of professional discipline but rather as practices indulged in by a frequent habitué at a club. Yet this is another reason why Adorno is impossible to assimilate to any system, even that of upper-class sensuousness: he literally defies predictability, turning his disaffected but rarely cynical eye on virtually everything within range.

Nevertheless Adorno, like Proust, lived and worked his entire life next to, and even as a part of, the great underlying continuities of Western society: families, intellectual associations, musical and concert life, and philosophical traditions, as well as any number of academic institutions. But he was always to one side, never fully a part of any. He was a musician who never had a career as one, a philosopher whose main subject was music. And unlike many of his academic or intellectual counterparts, Adorno never pretended to an apolitical neutrality. His work is like a contrapuntal voice intertwined with fascism, bourgeois mass society, and communism, inexplicable without them, always critical and ironic about them.

I think it is right therefore to see Adorno's extremely intense lifelong fixation on third-period Beethoven as the carefully maintained choice of a critical model, a construction made for the benefit of his own actuality as a philosopher and cultural critic in an enforced exile from the society that made him possible in the first place. To be late meant therefore to be late for (and refuse) many of the rewards offered up by being comfortable inside society, not the least of which was to be read and understood easily by a large group of people. On the other hand, people who have read and even admired Adorno sense in themselves a sort of grudging concession to his studious unlikability, as if he were not just a serious academic philosopher but an aging, disobliging, and even embarrassingly frank former colleague who, even though he has left one's circle, persists in making things hard for everyone.

I have spoken about Adorno in this way because around his quite amazingly peculiar and inimitable work a number of general characteristics of endings have coalesced. First of all, like some of the people he admired and knew—Horkheimer, Thomas Mann, Steuermann—Adorno was a worldly person, worldly in the French sense of *mondain*. Urban and urbane, deliberate, he was incredibly able to find interesting things to say about even so unassuming a thing as a semicolon or an exclamation mark. Along with these qualities goes the late style—that of an aging but mentally agile European man of culture who is absolutely not given to ascetic serenity or mellow maturity: there isn't much fumbling for references or footnotes or pedantic citations but always a very self-assured and well-brought-up ability to talk equally well about Bach and his devotees, about society and sociology.

Adorno is very much a late figure because so much of what he does militated ferociously against his own time. Although he wrote a great deal in many different fields, he attacked the major advances in all of them, functioning like an enormous shower of sulfuric acid poured over the lot. He opposed the very notion of productivity by being himself the author of an overabundance of material, none of it really compressible into an Adornian system or method. In an age of specialization he was catholic, writing on virtually everything that came before him. On his turf—music, philosophy, social tendencies, history, communication, semiotics—Adorno was unashamedly mandarin. There are no concessions to his readers, no summaries, small talk, helpful road signs, or convenient simplifying. And there is never any kind of solace or false optimism. One of the impressions you get as you read Adorno is that he is a sort of furious machine decomposing itself into smaller and smaller parts. He had the miniaturist's penchant for pitiless detail: he seeks out and hangs out the last blemish, to be looked at with a pedantic little chuckle.

It is the *Zeitgeist* that Adorno really loathed and that all his writing struggles mightily to insult. Everything about him, to readers who came of age in the 1950s and 1960s, was prewar and therefore unfashionable, perhaps even embarrassing, like his opinions on jazz and on otherwise universally recognized composers like Stravinsky and Wagner. Lateness for him equaled regression, from *now* to *back then*, when people discussed Kierkegaard, Hegel, and Kafka with direct knowledge of their work, not with plot summaries or handbooks. The things he wrote about he seems to have known since childhood and were not learned at university or by frequenting fashionable parties.

What is particularly interesting to me about Adorno is that he is a special twentieth-century type, the out-of-his-time late-nineteenth-century disappointed or disillusioned romantic who exists almost ecstatically detached from, yet in a kind of complicity with, new and monstrous modern forms—fascism, anti-Semitism, totalitarianism, and bureaucracy, or what Adorno called the administered society and the consciousness industry. He was very secular. Like the Leibnizian monad he often discussed with reference to the artwork, Adorno—and with him rough contemporaries like Richard Strauss, Lampedusa, and Visconti—is unwaveringly Eurocentric, unfashionable, and resistant to any assimilative scheme, yet he oddly reflects the predicament of ending without illusory hope or manufactured resignation.

Perhaps in the end it is Adorno's unmatched technicality that is so significant. His analyses of Schoenberg's method in *The Philosophy of New Music* give words and concepts to the inner workings of a formidably complex new outlook in another medium, and he does so with a prodigiously exact technical awareness of both mediums, word and tones. A better way of saying it is that Adorno never lets technical issues get in the way, never lets them awe him by their abstruseness or by the evident mastery they require. He can be more technical by elucidating technique from the perspective of lateness, seeing Stravinskian primitivism in the light of later fascist collectivization.

Late style is *in,* but oddly *apart* from the present. Only certain artists and thinkers care enough about their métier to believe that it too ages and must face death with failing senses and memory. As Adorno said about Beethoven, late style does not admit the definitive cadences of death; instead, death appears in a refracted mode, as irony. But with the kind of opulent, fractured, and somehow inconsistent solemnity of a work such as the *Missa Solemnis,* or in Adorno's own essays, the irony is how often lateness as theme and as style keeps reminding us of death.

TWO

Return to the Eighteenth Century

In my last chapter I began to discuss the phenomenon of late style, to which in a memorable fragment on Beethoven's third and final period Adorno gave extraordinarily dense and profound meaning. This idea about the coherence of "Spätstil," as Adorno called it, runs very consistently through many of his later studies of, for instance, Wagner's *Parsifal,* Schoenberg's last works, and so on. Partly because Adorno himself also represents an example of late style in the twentieth century, I began to study a group of twentieth-century artists, among them Richard Strauss, whose late works—*Capriccio,* the oboe concerto, the wind sonatas, the Second Horn Concerto, *Metamorphosis,* the *Four Last Songs*—impressed me for their undiminished power and yet strangely recapitulatory and even backward-looking and abstracted quality. Along with Strauss I have been interested in the later works of Genet, as well as those of the Italian director Luchino Visconti, particularly his 1963 adaptation of Lampedusa's *The Leopard,* a late novel if there ever was one.

The centrality of Strauss to my investigation of late style is especially acute. Glenn Gould rather extravagantly referred to him as the greatest musical personality of the twentieth cen-

tury, a claim that many contemporary musicians and critics
would not agree with. The by-now-canonical view of Strauss is
that after *Salomé* and *Elektra*—the latter was produced in
1909, the same year as Schoenberg's expressionistic mono-
drama *Erwartung*—he retreated into the sugary, relatively
regressive tonal, and intellectually tame world of *Der Rosenkavalier* (1911); from that point on he seems to have developed
very little if one compares him not only with the Second Viennese School but with less revolutionary contemporaries like
Hindemith, Stravinsky, Bartók, and Britten. True, in operas like
Ariadne auf Naxos (1916) and *Die Frau ohne Schatten* (1919),
he did advance beyond *Rosenkavalier,* but anything like the
radical power of his earlier scores, which had developed Wagner's chromaticism beyond even *Tristan,* he never approached,
much less achieved. Gould, who was as interested in Viennese
serialism as anyone, found this standard dismissal of Strauss
unacceptable, saying that the really interesting thing about
Strauss was that his career and his unequaled musical compe-
tence threw out of whack any simple chronological and developmental scheme. Indeed, Gould said, Strauss's immense gifts
and his prodigious output of arresting work for seven decades
make him

> more than the greatest man of music of our times. He is in my
> opinion a central figure in today's most crucial dilemma of
> aesthetic morality—the hopeless confusion that arises when
> we attempt to contain the inscrutable pressures of self guid-
> ing artistic destiny within the neat, historical summation of
> collective chronology. He is much more than a convenient
> rallying-point for conservative opinion. In him we have one of
> those rare, intense figures in whom the whole process of his-
> torical evolution is defied.[1]

About Strauss, Adorno is equally unrestrained, but very much against him. Adorno's monograph on the composer is one of his most coruscatingly sardonic, accusing him of manipulative egomania, of imitating and inventing rather than having emotions, of shameless self-presentation and nostalgic exaggeration. Strauss, according to Adorno, intended "to master music without submitting to its discipline: his ego ideal is now fully identified with the Freudian genital-character who is uninhibitedly out for his own pleasure. . . . His work has the atmosphere of the Grand Hotel of childhood, a palace accessible to money."[2] Next to the Grand Hotel, Adorno adds, stands the Grand Bazaar. As he gets going, Adorno is unstoppable, and the epithets and brilliant one-liners pour out. Strauss's music "simply cannot stay put, much like big entrepreneurs who are afraid of being ruined once the volume of business is no longer on the increase." His compositional style has no transitions in it: instead, "motifs—often of minimal importance—line up like pictures on an unending filmstrip." Completely, horrendously fluent, Strauss was "a composing machine," and what he actually wrote was "illusory" music "inasmuch as it is the semblance of life which does not exist" (RS 590, 591, 605).

And yet in the midst of this extremely unfriendly forest of epithets, Adorno still manages to find in Strauss something of value, albeit *negative* value because of the music's illusory quality. Perhaps I ought to say also that, as with much of his musical writing and by virtue of his fantastic gifts for ironic encapsulation, Adorno sometimes tends toward the incoherent or at least the deeply ambivalent. Having attacked Strauss for a large number of sins, Adorno suddenly discovers that the composer's fakery and slickness were useful in pointing to a "civilization before it unleashed its own barbarism and condemned itself as wrecked." Therefore "what must be salvaged is his idiosyncrasy, his hate of everything which, in his own words, was 'rigid' . . . He rebels against that sphere of the German spirit which self-righteously arrogates [to itself] the epithet 'substantial,' the indefatigable shopkeepers; he shoves it aside with a *dégoût* which would not have been unworthy of Nietzsche." Adorno goes on to admire in Strauss his capacities for resisting the regimented and for negating the negation, "fabricating an absent meaning out of the rubble of a reality which already rules over the genius who cannot survive in it" (RS 604–5).

In Strauss's extraordinary capacity for surprisingly and involuntarily recalling a lost childhood world, Adorno thus recovers the man's value: in his music senility and infancy "thumb . . . their nose at the censors." I think Adorno means more or less that Strauss escaped the rigors and the horrors of his time: his music was a throwback to an earlier age, as well as an index of how much his own had faded and decomposed. To understand Strauss therefore is "to listen for the murmur beneath the noise," since "the life which celebrates itself in this music is death." Finally, Adorno concludes, "solely in decline perhaps, is there a trace of what might be more than mortal: inextinguishable experience in disintegration" (RS 606).

This darkly metaphysical view of Strauss is very different from Gould's image of the man, blithely composing away with the real artist's indifference to chronology, the *Zeitgeist,* and the major advances in his own art. Gould makes no mention of Strauss's association with the Hitler period, through which he lived and, some would say, with which he has always been discreditably linked. Adorno does exactly the opposite, seeing in Strauss a throwback and a master technician, whose combined senility and infantilism (the words are Adorno's) were a sort of protesting resistance to the corrupt order all around. Only because he insulated himself in an aesthetic that was almost programmatically repressive could his music, with its astonishing technical mastery, make the case for being an admittedly problematic alternative to the prevailing cultural barbarism.

This is not the time for a detailed discussion of the whole Strauss question, as Michael Steinberg has called it, referring not only to his relationship with the Nazi Party and the German artistic establishment of the time, but also to the problems of his late music, which Steinberg unjustly calls consolatory and "neo-Biedermeier more than neoclassical."[3] Nevertheless it is worth mentioning that Steinberg's essay was written for an anthology of works about Strauss that was planned originally to accompany a six-day-long Strauss festival put on by and at Bard College during the summer of 1992. I attended most all of the dozen concerts that featured selections from all parts of Strauss's career as well as music by various contemporaries, including Schoenberg, Reger, Weill, Pfitzner, Busoni, Krenek, Ritter, Schreker, and Hindemith. Certainly in that highly varied context Strauss's music impressed one for its marvelously sustained quality and its always-interesting approach to whatever form Strauss happened to be composing in. Nothing I actually heard of the late music struck me as easily dismissible because, as Gould correctly notes, Strauss was always hugely competent and, among late German romantic composers, had a faculty that was unique, namely a "glorious harmonic infallibility." One didn't sense that faculty so strongly in most of the other composers performed at the Bard concerts because, as Gould also says, "Strauss was perhaps more concerned than any other composer of his generation with utilizing the fullest riches of late romantic tonality *within* the firmest possible formal disciplines."[4]

As others have noted, Strauss's late work communicates a sense of return and repose, to some extent greatly belied by the appalling events taking place all around him. Consider for

example *Capriccio,* Strauss's last opera, which he completed in
1941. It was first performed in 1942. There is something very
disconcerting about the fact that the opera was staged at a time
and in a place where a stone's throw away the extermination of
Europe's Jews was being planned. Yet none of this ruffles the
surface of the work; nor ought it to in any obvious way intrude
on any production of the work. Think of the opera as exhibit-
ing a hairline crack—like Henry James's golden bowl—that
could be rendered allusively, for instance, by revealing the back
of a butler's cutaway to be an SS uniform, or by having the
jacket of a Nazi uniform slung carelessly over one of the elegant drawing room chairs. In any event *Capriccio* is, like *Der
Rosenkavalier,* set in the eighteenth century. What is to be
made of this far-from-negligible fact.

The closer one looks at Strauss's interest in the eighteenth
century, the more important its hold on him seems. *Ariadne* was
originally planned with Hofmannsthal as a setting of Molière's
Bourgeois gentilhomme; well after most of the work was written, the two men decided to change the frame from the seventeenth to the eighteenth century, and from Paris to Vienna. Add
to that Strauss's lifelong interest in Mozart (the Second Wind
Sonata, the so-called *Symphonie für Bläser* [1945], is dedicated
to the spirit of Mozart) as well as his devotion to classical (in
Charles Rosen's sense of the word) forms, and one sees a massive and recurring presence of the eighteenth century in his
work that runs from the beginning to the end of the career.
Indeed we can go so far as to say that Strauss's late style in
effect *consecrates* this presence not only in *Capriccio* but in
the First and Second Wind Sonatinas, the Oboe Concerto, the
Duet Concertino for Clarinet and Bassoon, and *Metamorphosis.* It is this persistent embrace of and return to twentieth-
century versions of eighteenth-century idioms and forms that
distinguishes Strauss's style as we look at it in its wider cultural

setting, at a time when the modern movement in music simultaneously produced those more characteristically advanced or realistic styles we associate with dodecaphonism or serialism, polytonality, and in composers like Varèse, concrete music.

Yet Strauss is not alone in thus using the eighteenth century as a setting for his operatic works. For unless we recognize how relatively frequent that particular type of cultural appropriation is, we will then make the mistake of linking Strauss with John Corigliano's *The Ghosts of Versailles* (1991) in a unitary, essentially reactionary enterprise. At least three (four, if we include the *Dialogues des Carmélites*, which isn't quite on a level with the others) other major twentieth-century operatic works are concretely tied to the eighteenth century: Britten's *Peter Grimes* (1945), Stravinsky's *The Rake's Progress* (1951), and Kurt Weill's *The Threepenny Opera* (1928). Along with Strauss's three operas, they constitute an integral cultural formation that can be discussed together and distinguished from Corigliano's far less impressive contribution to the genre. *The Ghosts of Versailles* uses the eighteenth century politically as a way of disarming the audience, involving it in a trivial rather than an engaging spectacle, perhaps as a way of further defanging the very notion of opera itself, which is rendered as *only* an opera, peculiar, eccentric, irrelevant to the concerns of late-twentieth-century (imperial) America.

Corigliano and William Hoffman, his librettist, undertake a ghastly attempt to rewrite the history of the French Revolution, in which Beaumarchais the radical is shown to be in love with Marie-Antoinette, who turns out to be not the well-known symbol of an atrophied ancien régime but the opera's ingenue. Moreover the work's musical idiom is an unchallenging and unresolved one, whose personality wavers between imitation neoclassicism, musical comedy, and postserial modernism. All this plus a tasteless pastiche of eighteenth-century

Turkomania result in an appalling hodgepodge, incoherent in style, vulgar in display, and repellent in ideology. *The Ghosts of Versailles* is a contemporary return to a prerevolutionary past, a way of reassuring Americans that political disruptions can be ignored, or rectified by a sort of free-wheeling (if aesthetically incoherent) raiding of the past in a musical and dramatic idiom that seems anxious only to demonstrate its own power. By contrast, the Strauss, Stravinsky, Weill, and Britten operas involve music more deeply in issues of contemporary relevance, and by means of personal visions of the eighteenth century, they allow us new insights into that century as a cultural symbol. It is in that context that the late style of Richard Strauss is, I believe, most interestingly explored.

The Ghosts of Versailles also deserves to be contrasted with what, in his revisionary productions of Mozart's Da Ponte operas, Peter Sellars has been trying to do. An inordinate amount of newsprint has been expended on attacking Sellars for his settings of *The Marriage of Figaro, Don Giovanni,* and *Così fan tutte* in the Trump Tower, one of the New York barrios, and Despina's Diner respectively. While one can certainly discuss the failure or success of each of those realizations— I myself preferred Sellars's *Così* to the others—the fundamental point has been obscured, namely, that because of the whole idea of verisimilitude fostered by a far-too-steady diet of Italian *verismo* operas, we have forgotten that opera settings are ipso facto poetic and metaphoric, not automatically real or naturalistic. One can say, for instance, that Sellars's ideas for Mozart were too explicit, or too forcefully and unsubtly made, but not that he was taking liberties with eighteenth-century classics. Taking liberties is exactly what operas do, culturally speaking, and what Sellars underlined in his vision of the three operas was the extraordinary microscopic examination of social cruelty that Mozart undertook. By refusing to hide that concern under precisely the eighteenth-century curtsying and artifice exploited so cynically by Corigliano and his librettist Hoffman, Sellars was didactically, but also wittily, reminding a largely anesthetized twentieth-century American audience that operas could be brought into modernity, and not simply remain confined to a pseudo-museum arbitrarily created for them by institutions like the Metropolitan.

Once you begin to think about it, the choice of settings for operas is a fascinating topic. What distinguishes the majority of surviving and still-performed eighteenth-century operas— with the salutary exception of Gay's *The Beggar's Opera*—is the preponderance of subjects and settings chosen from classical antiquity; Handel and Gluck stand out, of course, but a great number of lesser figures also confirm this view. After Mozart, who occasionally avails himself of the classics, the practice diminished somewhat, although nineteenth-century composers like Berlioz and Weber and later Faure did continue it. With Mozart and Beethoven contemporary topics and settings began to emerge, and these in turn narrowed into a generally nationalist focus with Wagner, Smetana, Moussorgsky, Janáček, Bartók, Strauss, and many others in the late nineteenth and early twentieth centuries. The prevailing norms for opera production, after Bayreuth was established in 1876, were naturalistic and, as Verdi enviously remarked while he was preparing *Aida* for the Cairo Opera House, military; that is, conductors and directors begin to assert themselves more and more in the preemptory and often-dictatorial manner invented by Wagner for Bayreuth. Yet what Wagner brought, along with his interest in specifically Germanic myth and history, was a noticeable emphasis on the exotic, the picturesque, and the macabre, an infusion of the spectatorial and exhibitionistic element that had an overall distancing effect in the presentation of opera. In this respect earlier composers like

Meyerbeer and Halévy were, to Wagner's chagrin, the real pioneers, as much because they were successful as because such works at the same time had a very potent topical reference. Jane Fulcher has studied this paradoxical interplay of alienating spectacle and political intervention in the programs of the mid-nineteenth-century Paris Opera in her book *The Nation's Image*, subtitled *French Grand Opera as Politics and Politicized Art*, her notion being to insist that we "must understand social context" and to claim also that "the role that the theater played helped determine the experience and thus the utterance of this repertoire."[5]

The same claim cannot be made with as much certainty for the twentieth-century works I have been talking about. At one level, of course, operas like *Peter Grimes* and *Capriccio* are inextricably tied to the time and place of their first performance, as well as to the composer's social and aesthetic milieu. Yet what is truly different about these twentieth-century operas is that these works, while local on one level, are also extra-local in their subsequent careers. All of Strauss's operas were designed for subsequent performance elsewhere in Germany and Europe. *The Rake's Progress* is, I think, basically an international or cosmopolitan work. (Written by an expatriate Russian and an Englishman, it was first performed in Venice and cannot be said ever to have had a home base, so to speak.) And although *Peter Grimes* was first performed at the Sadler's Wells Opera in London, it was conceived originally by a pacifist, socialist, and homosexual expatriate Englishman while in New York, and it almost immediately began to have an international career. As for *The Threepenny Opera*, its record of change, transformation, and transmutation is quite dizzying, so that even though it is steeped in the atmosphere of 1920s Berlin, it is also a transnational work, for all its often confusing topicality (an English work using English characters set in the unmistakably German milieu exploited so ruthlessly by both Brecht and Weill).

These considerations, however, help us to understand the peculiar status of the eighteenth century represented in each opera. Even if the settings are highly specific, they are presented to the audience in such a way as actually to encourage their metamorphic universalization. This is emphatically the case with Stravinsky's *The Rake's Progress,* which is labeled a morality play by Stravinsky, a perspective underlined both by his production ideas and his choice of Hogarth's allegorical series as the prototype for the story invented by Auden and himself together. Every production of this opera that I have heard about or seen has been stylized, ironic, and self-conscious, as if to mirror Stravinsky's neoclassical music with its mocking allusions to *Don Giovanni* and the learned techniques of various other baroque composers. In completely avoiding the conventions of nineteenth-century opera, Stravinsky accentuates the contemporaneity of his work, calling attention to the artifice, mannerism, and capriciousness of a style that he created for dealing with the past. At the same time, as Donald Mitchell has said about Stravinsky's compositional mode, "the new part of the [musical] world that Stravinsky has made accessible to active creative feeling is no less than the past itself."[6] What emerges in *The Rake's Progress* is therefore the pastness of the past—to adapt from T. S. Eliot—as a subject for contemporary musical composition.

But why the eighteenth century as abstract and brief chronicle of the past? Here I must speculate, since in trying to establish a common motive for the choice of the eighteenth century in *Peter Grimes, Der Rosenkavalier, Capriccio,* and *The Rake's Progress,* a general supposition has to be looked for and, if possible, found. Note first of all that in each case, in addition to the opera's setting and specified time, the libretti are filled with concrete topical references. In *Capriccio,* for instance, Gluck is referred to several times, as is the eighteenth-century Parisian theater scene in which La Roche (the theater director) and Clairon (a star of the system) both function. In *Peter Grimes* details of the Suffolk coast fishing system predominate, as do the habits of that social entity that George Crabbe, in the poem on which the opera is based, called the Borough. Crabbe himself appears in the opera as a silent walk-on part, asked as a doctor by one of the characters to witness the depredations of the alienated and deeply distressed Peter Grimes. The same sort of thing is found in the other operas: a sprinkling of meticulously accurate period details whose presence in the libretto (especially in Hofmannsthal's incredibly profuse insertions into his text for *Rosenkavalier*), so to speak, enforces the eighteenth-century discipline.

I mention this to accentuate the composers' and librettists' insistence on marking the site and period of these operas with irreducible signs of the eighteenth century. To this add the use of eighteenth-century musical forms: for instance, the dance suite in *Capriccio,* the passacaglia in *Peter Grimes,* the Mozartian concert ensemble in *The Rake,* the ländler, waltzes, and staged arias in *Rosenkavalier,* and the ballads and chorales of *Threepenny Opera,* all of them reactions away from Wagnerian endless melody, with its sweeping, swirling formlessness and overwhelming impression of indistinctiveness and emotional turbulence. This putative defense against Wagner is less true of the early than of the late Strauss, but it is an important clue for our inquiry. Britten, Stravinsky, Weill, and Strauss, in wishing to avoid some of the powerful innovations introduced by Wagner, dissociate themselves not from his harmonic language—theirs would be unintelligible without his—but rather from a general attitude toward history prevalent in the nineteenth century that his operas—especially the *Ring* and those that followed—embody. This view sees history as incarnating a universal narrative, of the sort so regularly spun out by Wotan, Brünnhilde, and Erda in the *Ring:* history as a grand system to which everyone and every smaller narrative is subject. Myth, collective and tribal memory, national destiny: all these contribute to the power of the historical system animated by the *Ring,* as do, on a quotidian level, the actions and motivations of individual characters.

This system, far from being the product of Wagner's feverish and overwrought mind, is, as Stephen Bann has said in *The Clothing of Clio,* the accumulated result of many modes of representing history in nineteenth-century art, literature, and philosophy. Although Bann does not speak about music at all, his book can be construed as a running commentary on the invasion of nineteenth-century opera by history and historicization; for example, the representation of characters from the ancient world in *Aida* relies upon Egyptological discourse and discovery in ways unthinkable a generation earlier to Rossini in *Semiramide.* Herbert Lindenberger makes a similar point when he speaks about *Götterdämmerung* and *Boris Godunov* as operas of 1870, inflected by the ideology of late-nineteenth-century philology in the case of the former and by that of nationalist history in the case of the latter. Most of the great *verismo* works that are still in the repertory—like *Carmen* and *Cavalleria rusticana*—are historicized works that owe their sense of gritty realism to late-nineteenth-century ideas about history and an almost Darwinian sense of the social order.

To retreat into the eighteenth century is to go back before the French Revolution, that most universalizing and socially foundational of historical events, from which, in both England and France, writers like Scott, Michelet, Macaulay, and Quinet dated the onset of a particular national, social, and systematic emergent history. I don't want to say that Britten and Stravinsky are antihistorical in their operas, but their use of the eighteenth century permits them a different discipline and a different expression of history than they would otherwise have been committed to. Yet the prerevolutionary settings used by Strauss are quite different from those used by the three other major composers I've been discussing. Britten and Weill have in common a prerevolutionary view of society that is alienating and almost antagonistic, a collective worst self to be exposed and denounced in Weill's case, to be feared for its power to damage the vulnerable individual in Britten's. The pathos of Peter Grimes that Britten is centrally committed to expressing is that of a man surrounded by an uncomprehending populace, while he struggles to rise above his own history and circumstances into tragic vision. When Peter confronts his predicament in powerful operatic terms—alone with the orchestra in an anguished meditative aria—he is nonetheless hemmed in by the Borough and unable to get into his hut.

Grimes's suicide in the next act is projected logically from this scene. Yet so profoundly does Britten imagine the conflict in musical terms that we can quite easily see in it not only the metaphysical pathos of the preromantic sensibility (so deftly sketched by Crabbe) but the eighteenth-century concertato form of soloist and ensemble engaged individually and contrapuntally with each other.

Weill's method is simpler and less subtle. Like Gay and Stravinsky, he deals in allegorical types—the bandit, the beggar, the pawnbroker, the prostitute, the policeman—all of them freely manipulable by authors who confine them to predictable and unattractive postures expressly planned as rejections, even refutations of humanistic (as well as historical) theories about human perfectibility and improvement. The Rake's Progress and The Threepenny Opera are very different operas, different in intention and effect: I don't want to minimize that at all. Yet

I want also to stress how similarly they use character and scene to address the audience directly, to make self-consciously theatrical and metatheatrical points of the kind that nineteenth-century operas culminating in Wagner had totally banished. Two examples come to mind. The first is the finale to Act I of *The Threepenny Opera,* a trio for Polly and her parents, whose motif is, as Peachum puts it, "The world is poor and man's a shit." The second example is the final ensemble of *The Rake's Progress,* in which, according to Stravinsky's specifications, all the actors take off their masks and wigs and sing.

The Straussian eighteenth century is a considerably richer thing to study and, to return to Gould's description of Strauss's music, a remarkably sensitive indication of the man's "self-guiding artistic destiny," if one can really speak of such a thing so definitively and categorically. What is immediately striking about the eighteenth-century world that Strauss, Hofmannsthal, and Clemens Krauss represent is its overpowering wealth and privilege, demonstrations of which effectively structure the dramatic action of *Rosenkavalier* and *Ariadne.* Truly this world is prehistorical in its freedom from daily pressures and cares, and in its seemingly limitless capacity for self-indulgence, amusement, and luxury: and this too is a characteristic of twentieth-century late style. Although Gould doesn't say it, we can suppose that the image of an independent and completely self-enclosed musical career that Strauss's oeuvre seems to project is reinforced by the courtly conceits that stand at the center of his eighteenth-century operas, whose languid, perhaps even luxuriously trivial actions are commanded by the whims of a Maecenas, a princess, and a countess, as if snubbing the realistic norms not only of other operas but of other careers. *Luxe, calme, et volupté*—or so he would like it to seem, using the royalist and aristocratic exaggerations of the eighteenth century to signify the well-endowed man's ability to do as he pleases. Adorno mercilessly picks up on this in his essay about Strauss.

A closer look, however, reveals something far less free and easy. All three of the operas depict not so much a static scene as one constructed out of alternations between passages of the most exquisite, thoroughly harmonized lyricism and long passages of turbulent or capricious or sardonic activity. During the first act of *Rosenkavalier,* for instance, we have the ecstatic duet between Octavian and the Marschallin, giving way to Ochs and his machinations, as well as the frantic comings and goings of the levée. Yet Act I is centered musically by the Italian tenor's aria, which is commonly described as a parody or a caricature but in fact provides a harmonic anchor for the final canonic trio (which is in the same key, G flat) that resolves the conflict between the Marschallin's love for the younger Octavian, Octavian's loyalty to the Marschallin, and his love for Sophie.

It is as if Strauss were using music, or rather the music of music set in the eighteenth century, as a cadential harmonic island for the goings-on about music and art—this is especially true of *Ariadne* and *Capriccio*—operas dominated by people of wealth or a sort of whimsical power. After *Rosenkavalier* the specifically artistic island (which in *Ariadne* is a real island, too, that supplies the locale of the second act) becomes more and more metamusical, self-consciously and visibly retreating from the world of human affairs into a meditative, composed order of the kind Strauss was especially interested in projecting in his late period. Adorno associates this retreat with Proustian *mémoire involontaire:* in effect, it is much less random and more deliberate than that. In *Ariadne auf Naxos,* for instance, the exasperated Composer sings his paean to music after yet another intolerable intrusion into his plans for the opera *Ariadne* that he has composed but that the wealthiest man in

Vienna has demanded should be changed yet again. This paean can be compared with one the earliest utterances by Ariadne herself as she finds herself alone on Naxos, deserted by Theseus: she sings *"Es gibt ein Reich."*

In these two earlier operas, *Rosenkavalier* and *Ariadne,* the impassioned and yet lyrical poem or song delivered by the Italian tenor and the Composer respectively becomes a sort of preparation, a sort of dramatic *cantus firmus,* for the final scene, which is a concerted reiteration of it—the final trio in *Rosenkavalier,* the duet between Bacchus and Ariadne in *Ariadne auf Naxos.* Two decades after *Ariadne,* in *Capriccio,* Strauss employed a similar procedure, with a major difference, however. The setting of the opera is a palace outside Paris where the Countess and her brother entertain competing suitors, a poet and a musician, La Roche (the celebrated opera director), Clairon (an actress), and an Italian duo, a soprano and tenor, who establish a sort of artistic provenance for the opera in a long duet at the precise middle of the work. The action of Strauss's stage work has now retreated inward, so to speak, to an intramural level: the dramatic conflict is over whether in lyrical music the words or the music are more important, a conflict whose eighteenth-century Italian origins are referred to throughout the work, *primo le parole e dopo la musica,* or vice versa, as Olivier the poet and Flamand the composer debate the matter, vying for the countess's love, indefatigably. *Capriccio* is an extraordinarily rich and complex opera that can't possibly be done justice here, but two things about it relate back—in a different way, since it is now 1942, after all—to Strauss's use of the eighteenth century in *Ariadne* and *Rosenkavalier.* Olivier composes a sonnet, to which Flamand provides music: the work circulates throughout the opera in various forms, spoken, sung, instrumentally played through, and so on. In the final scene Countess Madeleine is alone, and as a way of somehow trying to decide between her two suitors she sings the sonnet, whose perfect eighteenth-century cadential strophes are enclosed in a late-nineteenth-century harmonic idiom.

The opera's final moments have her trying to decide between words and music, between Olivier and Flamand: "How can I tear this delicate fabric?" she asks herself. "Am I not myself part of its texture?" From such questions she abruptly moves out from her setting into the realm of the opera of which she is a character, and as she looks at herself in the mirror, she asks: "You mirror, showing a lovelorn Madeleine, ah, please advise me. Can you help me to find the ending for our opera?" *(Kannst du mir helfen, den Schluss zu finden für unser Oper?)* and adds "Is there one that isn't trivial?" *("Gibt es einen, der nicht trivial ist?")*

There is an earlier moment in the opera that should be looked at to make sense of these final moments. Not only do Olivier and Flamand quarrel over their primacy, but La Roche challenges them to put their talents to work in opera. "Let's make an opera together," says one of them, and at this moment Strauss allows the entire eighteenth-century setting to represent itself as well as the actual making of his own opera. Thus the eighteenth century becomes a metaphor for his work as a practicing composer, committed to tonal harmony, to artifice, to the métier of the working artist. La Roche assumes a dominating role in the debate (earlier he took a quite visible snooze onstage), angrily rising to impassioned declamation after Olivier and Flamand make fun of his newest production, a bombastic and expensive spectacle entitled *The Fall of Carthage*. "I am the real hero of the theater and of art," he says in the longest passage in the opera, one that is inexplicably ignored by critics. "I preserve the good things that have been written; the art of our fathers lies in my trust." It is easy to get the gist of his declaration: while the rest of you think about what to do, I do it; therefore, he says "pay your respects to my experience." He concludes with what he thinks should be written on his tombstone. Everyone agrees, and La Roche is universally acclaimed. Everyone except the Countess goes off with La Roche to write an opera, as one of them says, about ourselves and about "the happenings of this afternoon." Then the Countess finds herself alone, although Strauss takes care to add one last detail, the appearance of M. Taupe, the prompter, who has slept through the proceedings and is now looking for his absent cast. "Can this be a dream?" he asks. "Am I really awake?"

Strauss has gradually distilled the eighteenth century into a supple and resourcefully deployed symbol of his art, which he stages and redistributes throughout the expansive and yet strangely allusive action of *Capriccio*. La Roche is a man of the world, and Strauss is a productive and worldly composer who, despite the barbarism of Nazi Germany, is the keeper of the flame and of "the art of our fathers"—that is, of the musical tradition inherited from Haydn and Mozart. Although the long passage sung by La Roche is partly ironic and undercuts his pompous self-righteousness, Strauss must have been serious in believing that he and La Roche kept the flame lit, managing not to fall into unseemly political situations or, more to the point, not to stray into the numerous deviations opened up by musicians who left the tonal fold—like Webern, Berg, and Schoenberg.

In the more and more rarified atmosphere of *his* eighteenth century, Strauss can therefore read off and highlight his own stubborn artificiality as a musician, resolutely committed to a tonal language and traditional forms. The fact is that his vision of his world, through the privileged eighteenth-century ambiance he keeps coming back to, is not simply regressive and

reactionary: it is also a repeated assertion that such an aesthetically hospitable society—unlike the hostile world of Grimes's
Borough, or Stravinsky's Hogarthian London—can be lived in
and kept alive through the spectacular discipline that he, like
La Roche, has continuously practiced. Far from being an easily accessible and replicable world, the eighteenth century for
Strauss in his last years is a sort of sustained second nature, a
musical ethos so accomplished and so responsive to the atonal-
ity all around him as to acquire not just a utopian but an oddly
historical profile. You hear late Strauss, I think, as a counterpoint to Berg's *Lulu* or to Zimmerman's *Die Soldaten*. This
particular effect of sustaining a traditional line and yet also
allowing us to hear the interruptions of the outside world is, I
believe, what the final moment of *Capriccio* is all about.

Norman Del Mar has grouped the last works of Strauss's life
in what he calls "the Indian summer," suggesting a resurgence
of creative energy rivaling that of the earlier decades. Then,
after analyzing the *Four Last Songs,* he makes the following remarks about those extremely melancholy and affecting
orchestral songs: "The tiredness of great age in the presence of
impending and welcome death is not really sad but something
far deeper. It is the prerogative of great art that it arouses
nameless emotions which can tear us apart."[7] Inadvertently, I
think, Del Mar recalls Adorno ("in the history of art, late
works are the catastrophe"), although I also think that unlike
Adorno, Del Mar responds directly to Strauss's extraordinarily
accomplished musical staging, perhaps even theatricalization,
of an old man waiting for death. Clearly this is the main
intended effect of "Beim Schlafengehen" and "Im Abendrot,"
and most listeners probably cannot help feeling a noble sadness
coming over them as the long orchestral postlude gradually
winds down in E flat. In any event Del Mar doesn't explore
the "nameless emotions which can tear us apart." Strauss's

late style does indeed have an unsettling effect, however, and with an investigation of this I want to conclude this chapter. Like Adorno, Strauss is a figure of superannuation, a late-nineteenth-century essentially romantic composer living and writing well past his real period, exacerbating his already-unsynchronized idiom by moving stubbornly even further back in time to the eighteenth century. And with his ability so expertly to spin measure after measure of assured, even eloquent music in this regressive manner, Strauss is downright embarrassing: he shows little sign of anguish or discomfort, but when he does (as in the frankly elegiac and grieving *Metamorphosis*), an element of fluent and quasi-ornamental assertion enters in, which Adorno calls "the invention of the individual will acting entirely on its own . . . [hence] a will-to-style." Even more cruelly Adorno accuses Strauss's solemn moments of "having a conciliatory innocence of tone much like official speakers with classical citations" (RS 598, 599). If one recalls the appalling depredations of Germany during the war (perhaps with Mann's *Doktor Faustus* as a contrast to Strauss's conciliations), the embarrassment if anything increases.

When Adorno speaks scathingly of Strauss's "anachronistic backwardness," he really does miss the peculiar method of that trait and its amazingly engaging and consistent quality. First of all, Strauss's final works form a definite group within his oeuvre. They are escapist in theme, reflective and disengaged in tone, and above all written with a kind of distilled and rarefied technical mastery that is quite amazing. Here one ought to concentrate on the sheer difficulty of what Strauss attempts. The three big wind works are scored for fiendishly complex instrumental ensembles that almost defy graceful writing, and yet he pulls it off. *Metamorphosis* is scored in twenty-three separate lines for as many strings; it too is a technical tour de force. As for *Capriccio,* it is a concentrated epitome of the traditional composer's art, polished to a high degree of perfection; its characters, theme, and motivic structure are almost perversely circumscribed, as if to make the point overly plain that the composer is interested only in these relatively small-scale matters, not in anything more significant: the studied contrast with the advanced music of his time that I mentioned earlier intensifies the vulnerability and anomaly of its actual sound. The whole unbroken work in effect grows out of the string sextet in F with which the opera opens, and this *Vorspiel,* in its mellifluous, elegiac, and highly idiomatic mode, works less by assertion than by understated miniature—elegant, polite, and highly tonal.

Second, all the late instrumental works are not only technically brilliant, requiring great virtuosity to perform, but they are also curiously abstract and ornamental. Strauss seems very much given to an antiphonal effect when he combines two or more voices, and when he isn't writing the kind of soaring Olympian melody one finds, say, at the beginning of the Duet-Concertino, he gives his soloists a series of florid, almost arabesque lines best exemplified in the opening movement of the Oboe Concerto. *Metamorphosis* is the encyclopedic work of the late style, a very richly textured composition whose extremely ample scope furnishes the whole late period with a quasi-reference book of that period's characteristic musical manners.

All of this produces a studiously surface effect. Even the drama in *Capriccio,* as well as the world-weary *Last Songs,* is undramatic, free of contrast and real tension, unthreatening. And here we are at the unsettling and disconcerting core of this music: that from beginning to end it makes none of the emotional claims it should, and unlike late-style Beethoven with its fissures and fragments, it is smoothly polished, technically perfect, worldly, and at ease *as music* in an entirely musical world.

Perhaps the last thing one would normally say about Strauss's final works is that they are defiant, but I think that is exactly the word for them. Defiant and, except for their recognizably Straussian albeit now reduced method (the use of the 6/4 chord, the chamber music–like orchestration, the teasingly baroque as well as Viennese elements, and so on), unregimented, uncooptable into one or another of the accredited schools of the day. Finally, because a minimalist aesthetic is at work here, the music seems to stand aside: it renounces claims to metaphysical statement of the sort embodied in comparably eminent composers of the time, and it pliantly, agreeably, and immediately appears to an ear surprised, perhaps even shocked by the music's lack of complaint. There aren't so many options when a sense of lateness and incongruity comes over one, and Strauss's late-period music states the only appropriate option for him.

THREE

Così fan tutte at the Limits

Così fan tutte was the first opera I saw when I first came to the United States as a schoolboy in the early 1950s. The Metropolitan Opera production was by Lynn Fontanne and Alfred Lunt and, as I recall, was much celebrated as a brilliant yet faithful English-language rendition of a sparkling, beautiful, elegant opera that boasted an excellent cast—John Brownlee as Don Alfonso, Eleanor Steber and Blanche Thebom as the two sisters, Richard Tucker and Frank Guarrero as the young men, Patrice Munsel as Despina—and a fastidiously executed conception as an eighteenth-century court comedy. I remember a lot of curtsying, many lace hankies, elaborate wigs, acres of beauty spots, much chuckling, and all-around good fun, all of which seemed to go well with the very polished, indeed even superb singing by the ensemble. So powerful was the impression made on me by this *Così fan tutte* that most of the many subsequent performances of the work that I either saw or listened to seemed variations of that quintessentially classical production. When I saw the 1958 Salzburg production with Karl Böhm conducting and Schwarzkopf, Ludwig, Panerai, Alva, and Sciutti, I took it to be an elaboration of the Metropolitan realization.

Although I am neither a professional musicologist nor a

Mozart scholar, it has seemed to me that most, if not all, interpretations of the opera stress the kind of thing picked up on and magnified by Lunt and Fontanne—the work's effervescent, rollicking, courtly fun, the apparent triviality of its plot, its on the whole silly characters, and its astonishingly beautiful music, especially the ensembles. Though I have always wanted to see any production at all of Così fan tutte, I have also resigned myself to performances firmly grooved in *that* particular mode, which have never really convinced me that that mode is the right one for this superb yet elusive and somewhat mysterious opera. The only departure from the pattern was, of course, Peter Sellars's production of Così fan tutte, given along with the two other Mozart–Da Ponte collaborations; all three were originally staged at the now-defunct Pepsico Summer Festival in Purchase, New York, in 1986 and 1987. The great virtue of those productions was that Sellars swept away all the eighteenth-century clichés. Just as Mozart wrote these operas while the ancien régime was crumbling, he argued, contemporary directors should set them at a similar moment in our own time, with characters and settings that allude to the crumbling of the American empire as well as class deformations and personal histories that bear the marks of a society in crisis. Thus Sellars's version of Le nozze de Figaro takes place in the overblown luxury of the Trump Tower; Don Giovanni on a poorly lit street in Spanish Harlem, where dealers and junkies transact their business; Così fan tutte in Despina's Diner, where a group of Vietnam veterans and their girlfriends hang out, play tricky games, and get terrifyingly embroiled in feelings and self-discoveries that they are unprepared for and largely incapable of dealing with.

So far as I know, no one except Sellars has attempted so full-scale a revisionist interpretation of the three Da Ponte operas, which remain in the repertory as essentially courtly, classical eighteenth-century works. Even Salzburg's Patrice Chéreau production of *Don Giovanni*—despite its striking savagery and relentlessly obsessive pace—functions within what we take to be Mozart's theatrical idiom, recognizable as strictly eighteenth-century convention. What makes Sellars's productions of the three operas so powerful is that they put the viewer directly in touch with what is most eccentric and opaque about Mozart: the obsessive patterning in the operas, patterning that has little to do finally with showing that crime doesn't pay or that the faithlessness inherent in all human beings must be overcome before true union can occur. Moreover, Mozart's characters in *Don Giovanni* and *Così fan tutte* can indeed be interpreted not just as individuals with definable biographies and characteristics but as figures driven by forces outside themselves that they don't comprehend and make no serious effort to understand. These operas, in fact, are much more about power and manipulation than the directors allow; and individuality is reduced to a momentary identity in the impersonal rush of things. There is little room for providence, or for the heroics of charismatic personalities, although Don Giovanni himself cuts a defiant and dashing figure on a very limited scale. Compared with the operas of Beethoven, Verdi, or even Rossini, Mozart depicts an amoral Lucretian world in which power has its own logic, undomesticated by conditions of either piety or verisimilitude. Much as he seems to have looked down on Mozart's lack of seriousness, Wagner shared a similar worldview, which is one reason his characters in the *Ring, Tristan,* and *Parsifal* spend as much time as they do going over, re-narrating, and recomprehending the remorseless chain of actions in which they are imprisoned and from which there can be no significant escape. What is it that keeps Don Giovanni bound irrecusably to his licentiousness—exposed with such cold, quantitative precision by Leporello in *"Madamina, il cat-*

alogo questo"—or Don Alfonso and Despina to their schemes and fixings? Little in the operas themselves provides an immediate answer.

Indeed, I think Mozart tried to embody an abstract force that drives people by means of agents (in *Così fan tutte*) or sheer energy (in *Don Giovanni*) without the reflective consent of their mind or will in most instances. The intrigue in *Così fan tutte* is the result of a bet between Alfonso and Ferrando and Guglielmo, inspired neither by a sense of moral purpose nor by ideological passion. Ferrando is in love with Dorabella, Guglielmo with Fiordiligi; Alfonso bets that the women will be unfaithful. A subterfuge is then enacted: the two men pretend that they have been called off to war, then come back in disguise and woo the girls. As Albanian (i.e., Oriental) men, the two attempt to seduce each other's fiancé. Guglielmo quickly succeeds with Dorabella; Ferrando needs more time, but he too is successful with Fiordiligi, who is clearly the more serious of the two sisters. Alfonso is helped in the plot by Despina, a cynical maid who assists in her mistresses' downfall, although she does not know of the bet between the men. Finally the plot is exposed, and the women are furious, but they return to their lovers even though Mozart does not specify exactly whether the pairs remain as they were at the outset.

As many commentators have noted, the opera's plot has antecedents in various "test" plays and operas, and as Charles Rosen correctly says, it resembles "demonstration" plays written by Marivaux among others. "They demonstrate—prove by acting out—psychological ideas," Rosen adds, "and 'laws' that everyone accepted, and they are almost scientific in the way they show precisely how these laws work in practice."[1] He goes on to speak of *Così fan tutte* as "a closed system," an interesting if insufficiently examined notion that does in fact apply to the opera.

We can learn a good deal about *Così fan tutte* in the late-eighteenth-century cultural setting by looking at Beethoven's reactions to the Da Ponte operas, which he, as an Enlightenment enthusiast, seems always to have regarded with a certain amount of discomfort. Like many critics of Mozart's operas, Beethoven was—so far as I have been able to discover—curiously silent about *Così fan tutte.* To generations of Mozart admirers, including Beethoven, the opera seems to refuse the kind of metaphysical, or social, or cultural significance that Kierkegaard and other luminaries found readily in *Don Giovanni, Die Zauberflöte,* and *Figaro.* There therefore seems very little to say about it. Most people concede that the music is extremely wonderful, but the unsaid implication is that it is wasted on a silly story, silly characters, and an even sillier setting. Significantly enough, Beethoven seems to have thought *Die Zauberflöte* the greatest of Mozart's works (mainly because it was a German work), and he is quoted by Ignaz von Seyfried, Ludwig Rellstab, and Franz Wegeler separately as expressing his dislike of *Don Giovanni* and *Figaro;* they were too trivial, too Italian, too scandalous for a serious composer. Once, however, he expressed pleasure at *Don Giovanni*'s success, although he was also said not to have wanted to attend his great older contemporary's operas because they might make him forfeit his own originality.

These are the contradictory feelings of a composer who found Mozart's work as a whole unsettling and even disconcerting. Competitiveness is a factor, but there is something else: it is Mozart's uncertain moral center, the absence in *Così fan tutte* of a specific humanistic message of the kind that *Die Zauberflöte* is so laboriously explicit about. What is still more significant about Beethoven's reactions to Mozart is that *Fidelio,* his only opera, can be interpreted as a direct, and a somewhat desperate, response to *Così fan tutte.* Take one small but certainly telling example: Leonore's appearance at the outset disguised as a young man who comes to work as Rocco's assistant at the prison and engages the amorous attentions of Rocco's daughter Marzelline. You could say that Beethoven has picked up a bit of the *Così* plot, in which the disguised lovers return to Naples and proceed to advance on the wrong women, Ferrando coming on to Fiordiligi, Guglielmo on to Dorabella. No sooner does the intrigue start up than Beethoven puts a stop to it, revealing to the audience that young Fidelio is the ever-faithful and constant Leonore, come to Don Pizarro's prison in order to assert her fidelity and her *amour conjugal*, to use the exact title of Bouilly's work from which Beethoven took some of his material.

Nor is this all. Leonore's central aria, *"Komm Hoffnung,"* is full of echoes of Fiordiligi's *"Per pietà, ben mio perdona"* in Act II of *Così*, which she sings as a last, forlorn plea to herself to remain constant and to drive away the dishonor she feels might be overcoming her as she suffers (and perhaps slightly enjoys) the impress of Ferrando's importuning. *"Svenerà quest'empia voglia, l'ardir mio, la mia costanza. Perderà la rimembranza che vergogna e orror mi fa."* (I'll rid myself of this terrible desire with my devotion and love. I'll blot out the memory that causes me shame and horror.) Memory for her is what she must hold on to, the guarantee of her loyalty to her lover, for if she forgets, she loses the ability to judge her present, timidly flirtatious behavior for the shameful wavering it really is. And memory is also that which she must banish as she recalls what she is ashamed about: her trifling with her real but absent lover Guglielmo. Mozart gives her a noble, horn-accompanied figure for this avowal, a melody to be echoed as to key (E major) and instrumentation (also horns) in Leonore's great appeal to hope, *"Lass den letzten Stern der Müden nicht erbleichen"* (Let this last star for the weary not be extinguished). But Leonore actually depends on hope and love; she does not doubt them, and although like Fiordiligi she has a secret, hers is an honorable one. There is no wavering, no doubting or timidity in Leonore, and her powerful aria, with its battery of horns proclaiming her determination and resolve, seems almost like a reproach to Fiordiligi's rather more delicate and troubled musings. Finally, Fiordiligi ends her aria on a note of regret since she has already embarked on her course of betrayal, whereas of course Leonore is beginning her own ordeal of constancy and redemption on behalf of her as-yet-disappeared husband.

There is no way at all of actually proving any of this. Yet the differences in tone between *Così* and *Fidelio* are so striking and the resemblances so marked that it would be interpretively irresponsible not to think of the later opera as Beethoven's sturdy response, half conscious and half deliberate, to Mozart's disruption of the acceptable bourgeois ideal. It isn't right, on the other hand, to consider Beethoven as a naïve missionary, hymning the virtues of true virtue and connubial bliss without doubt or even skepticism. For despite its programmatic enlistment in the ranks of the constant and the faithful, *Fidelio* is somewhat desperate in its assertions and quite uncertain, even minimal, in its certainties. Florestan, for example, is supposed to stand for principle and freedom, yet he tells us only that he once spoke the truth and was since punished for it: *"Wahrheit wagt' ich kühn zu sagen, und die Ketten sind mein Lohn."* (I boldly dared to speak the truth, and these chains are my reward.) He and Leonore express their passion for each other as a nameless joy—as if they can say nothing about it—and in the final apotheosis, when Don Ferrando gives the order for the prisoners' release, the martial, pounding accents of orchestra and chorus, with the C major underlined many times in a paroxysm of clangorous chords and static harmonies, convey the impression that Beethoven is trying to keep the victory on stage a bit longer so that it might last. Once the music stops, no one has anything more to say. All is not really well, and not everything has been fixed: the brief righting of wrongs is but a temporary respite from the darkness. The hastily assembled, embarrassed crowd that for some time has lived with and near Pizzaro's dungeons uncomplainingly shouts its faith in freedom and justice, but it isn't really convincing: why did things endure as long as they did, Beethoven seems to have naggingly asked himself, especially if virtue is as strong as the opera suggests it is? Earlier, the famous B-flat trumpet call that penetrates the prison's darkness and saves both Florestan and Leonore from Pizzaro's weapon is providential, but it remains outside the action, outside the sordid world of faithlessness and evil that (inadvertently perhaps) Beethoven spends so much time embodying and trying simultaneously to refute.

Doubtless these are issues of importance to Beethoven that he wrestled with in *Fidelio* independently of *Così*, but I think we have to grant that something about Mozart's operatic world in his mature and greatest works (with the exception of *Die Zauberflöte*) kept bothering Beethoven. Partly, of course, it was their sunny, comic, and southern setting, which amplifies their underlying critique and implied rejection of the middle-class virtue that seems to have meant so much to Beethoven. Even *Don Giovanni,* the one Da Ponte opera that has come in for twentieth-century reinterpretation that has turned it into a "northern" psychodrama of neurotic drives and transgressive passions, is essentially more unsettlingly powerful when enacted as a comedy of heedlessness and enjoyable insouciance. The style of famous twentieth-century Italian Dons like Ezio Pinza, Tito Gobbi, and Cesare Siepi prevailed until the 1970s, after which their characterizations gave way to those of Thomas Allen, James Morris, Francesco Furlanetto, and Samuel Ramey, who represent the Don as a dark figure anticipating his readings in Kierkegaard and Freud. *Così fan tutte* is even more aggressively "southern" in that all of its Neapolitan characters are depicted as being shifty, pleasure-centered, and with the exception of a brief moment here and there, selfish and relatively free of guilt, even though of course what they do is, by *Fidelio*'s standards, patently reprehensible.

Thus the earnest, heavy, and deeply serious atmosphere of *Fidelio* can be seen as a reproach to *Così*, which, for all its ironies and beauties so well described by recent critics like Rosen and Scott Burnham, is grippingly without any kind of gravity at all. When the two pseudo-Oriental suitors are repulsed by Fiordiligi and Dorabella at the end of Act I, they drag the sisters into a broadly comic, false suicide scene; what transpires is based on the ironic disparity between the women's earnest concern for the men, and the two suitors' amused playacting; Despina's pretending to be a Mesmer-like *"medico"* whom the women can't understand *("parla un linguaggio che non sappiamo")* is added on for good measure. Genuine emotion is thus undercut by the ridiculousness of what is going on. In Act II, where the disguises and play-acting advance quite significantly into the emotions of the four main characters, Mozart extends the joke even further. The result is that the four do fall in love again, though with the wrong partners, and this undermines something very dear to Beethoven, constancy of identity. Indeed, all the characters in *Fidelio* are rigorously circumscribed in their unvarying essence: Pizarro as unyielding villain, Florestan as champion of good, Fernando as emissary of light, and so forth. This is at the opposite pole from *Così*, where disguises, and the wavering and wandering they foster, are the norm, and where constancy and stability are mocked as impossible. Despina puts it quite explicitly in Act II: *"Quello ch'è stato è stato, scordiamci del passato. Rompasi ormai quel laccio, segno di servitù.*" (What's done is done, and the less said, the better. Let's break all ties to the past, as a symbol of servitude.)

Still, we need to look at Così *fan tutte* as an opera whose strange lightheartedness hides, or at least underplays, an inner system that is quite severe and amoral in its workings. I do not at all want to say that the work must not be enjoyed as the brilliant romp that in many ways it surely is. The critic's role, however, is to try to lay bare what it is that Mozart and Da Ponte were trying to intimate through their merry tale of deceit and displaced love. R. P. Blackmur quite rightly says that "the critic brings to consciousness the means of performance." I shall therefore try to elucidate the way in which Così *fan tutte* is at its concealed limits a very different work than its rollicking exterior and sublime music suggests, although part of the joy is how, in bringing to consciousness the means of Mozart and Da Ponte's performance, we appreciate and derive pleasure from the contradictory ways the opera unfolds before us in the theater.

Thanks to Alan Tyson's careful research, we now know that Mozart composed the ensembles of Così before he took on the arias and even the overture. This sequence corresponds to the opera's concentration on relationships between characters rather than on the brilliant individuals of earlier operas like *Figaro* or *Don Giovanni*. Of the three Da Ponte operas, Così *fan tutte* is not only the last and, in my opinion, the most complex and eccentric, but also the most internally well organized, the most full of echoes and references, and the most difficult to unlock, precisely because it goes further toward the limits of acceptable, ordinary experiences of love, life, and ideas than either of its two immediate predecessors. The reasons for this, and indeed for *Così*'s opacity and even resistance to the kind of political and intellectual interpretive analysis that *Figaro* and

Don Giovanni generally permit, are partly to be found in Mozart's life and times in 1789–90, while he was at work on *Così*. But they are also to be found in the way Mozart and Da Ponte created the work together, without a well-known play or a legendary figure to provide them with a framework and directions. *Così* is the result of a collaboration, and its dynamics, the symmetrical structure of its plot, and the echoic quality of much of its music are internal as well as necessary to its composition, not imported into or imposed on it by an outside source.

Many of the numbers of Act I, for example, were written by Mozart to emphasize how the characters think, act, and sing in pairs; their lines generally imitate one another and recollect lines sung earlier. Mozart seems to have wanted us to feel we are inside a closed system in which melody, imitation, and parody are very difficult to separate from one another. This is superbly in evidence in the Act I sextet, which enacts a sort of miniplay in which Alfonso draws Despina, then the two disguised men, then the two women into his plot, all the while commenting on the action, as he also allows Despina to comment. The whole number (written in the opera's basic key of C major) is a dizzying maze of advance and expostulation, statement, echo, and inversion that rivals anything Mozart ever wrote. It simply sweeps aside the last trace of any sense of stability and gravity that we have so far been able to hold on to.

Yet to encounter *Così* today, either on disc or in the theater, is with few exceptions to risk missing how carefully Mozart intended all of this. Opera is experienced in the theater as a basically undramatic, albeit theatrical and extravagant, form. Most spectators do not understand the language, and if they do they cannot understand the singers; in addition, *Così* has an aggressively inconsequential plot that is enacted by characters who seem to have no interesting past to unravel or expose, and no encumbering relationships that claim their loyalty and the investment of their emotions. Surface seems to be all, except for the music, which is dazzling. The social framework, and what fifty years ago Adorno called the regression of hearing, operate to sever music from drama and language: we tend to think of opera as a series of arias or tunes connected to one another by a generally stupid or melodramatic or unreal kind of story, in which we listen to the music in spite of the ridiculous and probably irrelevant goings-on on the stage. Some composers, Wagner most prominently, carry with them an aura of profundity or at least significance of the kind that Wagner himself took great pains in his prose works to elaborate and to ascribe to his operas. But not even many Wagnerites carry his ideas in their mind when they see a performance of *Lohengrin* or *Tristan* at the opera house: those performances are part of what is called "opera," a not-quite-rational, emotive form that is less serious than drama and of somewhat more consequence than musical comedy. What seems to me the one absolutely central and radical question about opera is the question "Why do these people sing?" Yet in the conditions under which operas are given today—as hugely expensive, lumbering projects curatorially rendered as pertaining to a distant, largely irrecoverable past and to an eccentric, privileged, and unserious present—the question can scarcely be posed, much less answered.

Così fan tutte presents special problems today when mindless productions resolutely stand against our own contemporary world of ideas and politics, reflecting only the tastes and prejudices of a small coterie that has decided to keep opera frozen in a harmless little box that can offend neither audiences nor corporate sponsors. To come to terms with *Così* is first of all to be reminded that when it was first performed in Vienna on January 26, 1790, it was a contemporary opera, not a "classic," as it has become. Mozart worked at it during the first part of 1789, at a time when he had just passed through a period of great difficulty. Andrew Steptoe discusses the circumstances of the composer's life at the time of *Così*'s composition with great insight and tact, although like all other commentators he is obliged to rely on speculation, since the actual information we seem to have is unusually sparse. Steptoe first of all points out that after *Don Giovanni* in 1787 "Mozart's personal health and financial security deteriorated." Not only did a German tour he undertook fail, but he seems to have passed through "a loss in creative confidence," composing very few works and leaving an unusual number of fragments and unfinished pieces. In particular he had difficulties with the quartets he was writing for Kaiser Friedrich Wilhelm, which he did not complete for over a year.[2]

We do not really know why he took up work on *Così fan tutte*, although Steptoe volunteers (correctly I think) that the piece "was therefore located at a pivotal moment, and must have been seized upon by the composer both as an artistic challenge and a golden opportunity to recoup financially" (MDO 209). The score that he finally did produce bears the marks, I believe, of other aspects of his life in 1789. One (referred to by Steptoe) is his wife Constanze's absence for a rest cure in Baden while he worked on the opera. While there she "displayed improprieties" that prompted a letter from Mozart casting himself as the constant one, his wife as the flighty, embarrassing partner who needed to be *reminded*—the theme of remembering and forgetting is basic to *Così*—of her position and domestic status:

> Dear little wife! I want to talk to you quite frankly. You have
> no reason whatever to be unhappy! You have a husband who

loves you and does all he possibly can for you. As for your foot, you must just be patient and it will surely get well again. I am glad indeed when you have some fun—of course I am— but I do wish that you would not sometimes make yourself so cheap. In my opinion you are far too free and easy with N.N. . . . Now please remember that N.N. is not half so famil- iar with other women, must have been misled by your behav- ior into writing the most disgusting and most impertinent sottise which he put into his letter. A woman must always make herself respected, or else people will begin to talk about her. My love! Forgive me for being so frank, but my peace of mind demands it as well as our mutual happiness. Remember that you yourself once admitted to me that you were inclined to comply too easily. You know the consequences of that. Remember too the promises you gave to me. Oh, God, do try, my love! (MDO 87–88)

How important Mozart's own almost Archimedean sense of stability and control was in dealing with Constanze is remarked by Steptoe, who argues that because Mozart did not believe in "blind romantic love," he went on to "satirize it mercilessly (most notably in Così fan tutte)." But the letters from the Così period quoted by Steptoe relate a more compli- cated story. In one, Mozart tells Constanze how excited he is at the prospect of seeing her, then adds, "If people would see into my heart, I should almost feel ashamed." We might then expect him to say something about seething passions and sensual thoughts. Instead he continues: "To me, everything is cold—cold as ice" (MDO 90). And then he notes that "every- thing is so empty." In a subsequent letter, also quoted by Step- toe, Mozart speaks again of "feeling—a kind of emptiness, which hurts me dreadfully—a kind of longing, which is never satisfied, which never ceases, and which persists, nay rather increases daily" (MDO 90). In Mozart's correspondence there are other letters of this sort that characterize his special combination of unstilled energy (expressed in the sense of emptiness and unsatisfied longing that increases all the time) and cold control: these qualities seem to me to have a particular relevance to the position of *Così fan tutte* in his life and oeuvre.

Figaro and *Don Giovanni* belong to the same group as *Così*, of course, but whereas they are expansive, explicit, and intellectually and morally transparent, *Così* is concentrated, full of implicit and internalized characteristics, and morally and politically limited, if not opaque: the third Da Ponte opera is also, relatively speaking, a late work, rather than just a mature one as its predecessors were. The opera's score is not only structured by the ensembles but looks back to earlier works and is full of "thematic reminiscences," as Steptoe calls them. At one point in Act I (Dorabella's accompanied recitative *"Ah, scostati"*), the orchestra suddenly plays the rapid scale passages associated with the Commendatore in *Don Giovanni*. Mozart's use of counterpoint gives the music added substance, so that in the E-flat canon in the second-act finale one experiences not only a remarkable sense of rigor but also a special ironic expressiveness well beyond the words and the situation. For as the lovers have finally worked their way around to the new reversed pairing, three of them sing polyphonically of submerging all thought and memory in the wine they are about to drink, while only one, Guglielmo, remains disaffected— he had greater faith in Fiordiligi's power to resist Ferrando but has been disproved—and he stands outside the canon; he wishes that the women *("queste volpi senza onor")* would drink poison and end the whole thing. It is as if Mozart wanted the counterpoint to mirror the lovers' embarrassment in a closed polyphonic system, and also to show how even though they think of themselves as shedding all ties and memories, the music, by its circularity and echoic form, reveals them to be bound to one another in a new and logically consequent embrace.

Such a moment is unique to *Così fan tutte*: it depicts human desire and satisfaction in musical terms as essentially a matter of compositional control directing feeling and appetite into a logical circuit that allows no escape and very little elevation; Guglielmo's bad-tempered, sour line further negates the consummation implied in the words. But the whole opera—plot, characters, situation, ensembles, and arias—tends to such a cluster as provided here because it is derived from the movement of two intimate couples, two men and two women, plus two "outside" characters, coming together in various ways, then pulling apart, then coming together again, with several changes along the way. The symmetries and repetitions are almost cloying, but they are the substance of the opera. We know very little about these figures; no traces of a former life adhere to them (unlike the characters in *Figaro* and *Don Giovanni*, who are steeped in earlier episodes, entanglements, and intrigues); their identities exist in order to be tested and exercised as lovers, and once they have gone through one full turn so that they become the opposite of what they were, the opera ends. The overture, with its busy, clattering, roundlike themes, catches this spirit quite perfectly. Remember that Mozart wrote it after he had finished most of the main body of the opera— that is, after the schematic character of what he was elaborating had impressed itself on his mind.

Only one figure, Don Alfonso, stands apart: his is the only activity that begins before the opera opens—in the opening trio, which seems to be the continuation of an argument already begun, Ferrando and Guglielmo refer to Alfonso's antecedent comment that *"detto ci avete che infide esser ponno"* (you've already told us they could be untrue)—and it continues uninter-

ruptedly to the very end. Who is he really? He certainly belongs
to the line of senior authority figures who dot Mozart's life and
works. Remember the Commendatore in *Giovanni,* or Sarastro
in *Die Zauberflöte,* or even Bartolo and Almaviva in *Figaro.*
Yet Alfonso's role is different from the others in that he seeks to
prove not the underlying moral fiber but the inconstancy and
unfaithfulness of women; and he succeeds, initiating the four
lovers into a life of reason and undeceived love. In the final
ensemble, when the women denounce him as the man who
misled them and managed their fall, Alfonso responds without a trace of regret: what he has done, he says, is to have
undeceived them, and this, he adds, puts them more under
his command. *"V'ingannai, ma fu l'inganno disinganno ai
vostri amanti, che più saggi omai saranno, che faran quel ch'io
vorrò"* (I deceived you, but my deception was to undeceive
your lovers. From now on they'll both be wiser, and they'll do
just as I say). Join hands, he says, so that all four of you can
laugh, as I have laughed and will laugh again. It is interesting
and not entirely a coincidence that what he sings contains
striking anticipations of *Die Zauberflöte,* an opera that Mozart
seems to have written as a more morally acceptable version of
the same demonstration or test story used in *Così fan tutte.*
Whereas in *Così* constancy *does not* win out, in *Die Zauberflöte* it does.

Like Sarastro, Don Alfonso is a manager and controller of
behavior, although unlike Sarastro he shows neither solemnity nor high moral purpose in what he does. Most accounts
of the opera scarcely pay attention to him, and yet in the
unguardedly amoral world of *Così* he is not only a crucial and
indeed the pivotal figure but also a fascinating one. His many
references to himself—actor, teacher, scholar (the various Latin
tags and classical references suggest a good education), plotter,
courtier—do not directly allude to the one thing he seems

above all others to be: a mature libertine, someone who has had lots of worldly sexual experience and now wishes to direct, control, manipulate the experience of others. In this respect he resembles an amiable schoolmaster, a military strategist, and a philosopher: he has seen much in the world and is more than able to stage another drama of the sort he has presumably lived through himself. He knows in advance what conclusion he will come to, so the action of the opera furnishes him with few surprises, least of all about how women behave. Plowing the sea, sowing on sand, trying to ensnare the wind in a net: these impossibilities define the limits of Alfonso's reality, and they accentuate the element of radical instability in which as a teacher of lovers, and a practiced lover himself, he lives, and that his agitated little D-minor passage so effectively renders. This apparently does not prevent him from enjoying both the experience of loving and the experience of proving his ideas that he sets up in order to demystify love for his four young friends.

I do not want to suggest that Don Alfonso is anything other than a comic figure. But I do want to argue that he stands very close to a number of cultural and psychological actualities that meant a great deal to Mozart especially but also to other relatively advanced thinkers and artists of the time. Consider first the unmistakable progression in Mozart's operatic invention from Figaro to Don Giovanni to Don Alfonso. Each in his own way is unconventional and iconoclastic, although only Don Alfonso is neither punished, like Don Giovanni, nor in effect domesticated, as Figaro is. To have discovered that the stabilities of marriage and the social norms habitually governing human life are inapplicable because life itself is as elusive and inconstant as his experience teaches makes of Don Alfonso a character in a new, more turbulent, and troubling realm, one in which experience repeats the same disillusioning patterns without relief. What he devises for the two pairs of lovers is a game in which human identity is shown to be as protean, unstable, and undifferentiated as anything in the actual world. Not surprisingly, then, one of the main motifs in *Così fan tutte* is the elimination of memory so that only the present is left standing. The structure of the plot, with its play-within-a-play abstractions, enforces that: Alfonso sets up a test, which separates the lovers from their past and their loyalties. Then the men assume new identities and return to woo and finally win the women; Despina is also brought in, although she and Alfonso remain emotionally detached from the two central pairs. The net effect is that Ferrando and Guglielmo enter into their new roles as much as the women, take seriously their charge as lovers, and in the process prove what Alfonso knew all along. Yet Guglielmo is not so easily resigned to Fiordiligi's apparent fickleness and therefore remains for a time outside Alfonso's circle of happy, and deceived, lovers; despite his bitterness, however, he rallies around to Alfonso's thesis, given full articulation in the opera now for the first time. Note here that Alfonso's statement is in C major, the basic key of the opera; its climax is the rudimentary harmonic progression (I, IV, V, I) that is the germ of *Così fan tutte;* and its style is both academic and—for Mozart—extremely plain.

This is a late moment in the opera. Alfonso has been biding his time before putting things so flatly, in so unadorned and reductive a manner. It is as if he, and Mozart, needed Act I to set up the demonstration and Act II to let it spin itself out, before he could come forward with this conclusion, which is also the musical root, finally revealed, of the opera. In this respect Alfonso represents the standpoint not just of a jaded, illusionless man of the world but also of an indefatigable practitioner and rigorous, albeit only partially involved, teacher of his views, a figure who apparently needs subjects and space for his demonstrations, even though he knows in advance that the pleasures he sets up are far from new. They may be exciting and amusing, but they simply confirm that about which he has no doubt.

In this respect Don Alfonso resembles an understated version of his near-contemporary the Marquis de Sade, a libertine who, as Foucault describes him memorably,

> while yielding to all the fantasies of desire and to each of its furies, can, but also must, illumine their slightest movement with a lucid and deliberately elucidated representation. There is a strict order governing the life of the libertine: every representation must be immediately endowed with life in the living body of desire, every desire must be expressed in the pure light of representative discourse [in this case in Act II, the language or discourse of love]. Hence the rigid sequence of "scenes" (the scene in Sade is profligacy subjected to the order of representation) and, within the scenes, the meticulous balance between the conjugation of bodies and the concentration of reasons.[3]

We recall that in the opera's first number Alfonso speaks, he says, "ex cathedro," a man with gray hair and long experience: we are to assume, I think, that having yielded to desire in the past he is now ready to illuminate his ideas "with a lucid and deliberately elucidated representation," which of course is the comedy he imposes on Guglielmo and Ferrando. The plot of *Così* is a rigid sequence of scenes, all of them manipulated by Alfonso and Despina, his equally cynical helper, in which sexual desire is, as Foucault suggests, profligacy subjected to the order of representation—that is, the enacted tale of lovers being schooled in an illusionless yet exciting love. When the game is revealed to Fiordiligi and Dorabella, they accept the truth of what they have experienced, and in a conclusion that has troubled interpreters and directors with its coy ambiguity, they sing of reason and mirth without any specific indication at all from Mozart that the two women and two men have returned to their original lovers.

Such a conclusion opens up a troubling vista of numerous further substitutions, with no tie, no identity, no idea of stability or constancy left undisturbed. Foucault speaks of this cultural moment as one in which language retains the capacity to name but can only do so in a "ceremony reduced to the utmost precision . . . and extends it to infinity": the lovers will go on finding other partners, since the rhetoric of love and the representation of desire have lost their anchors in a fundamentally unchanging order of Being. Since "our thought is so brief, our freedom so enslaved, our discourse so repetitive . . . we must face the fact that that expanse of shade below is really a bottomless sea."[4] It is against this rather dreadful vista that Mozart permits only one character, Guglielmo, to rage openly: this is the import of his harsh and yet aggressively charming patter aria, *"Donne mie, la fate a tanti."*

Don Alfonso is responsible for that rage, a parodic Virgil leading young, inexperienced men and women into a world stripped of standards, norms, and certainties. He speaks the language of wisdom and sagacity allied to an (admittedly) small-scaled and limited vision of his power and control. The libretto contains plenty of classical references, but none of them refer to the Christian or Masonic deities that Mozart elsewhere seems to have venerated. (He became a Mason in 1784.) Don Alfonso's natural world is in part Rousseau's, stripped of sanctimonious piety, volatile with fancy and caprice, made rigorous with the need to experience desire without palliatives or conclusion. Even more significantly for Mozart, Don Alfonso is only the second authority figure in his operas to appear after the death of Leopold in 1787; given some urgency by his father's death, the terrifying Commendatore in *Don Giovanni* embodies the stern, judgmental aspect of Leopold's relationship with his son (discussed by Maynard Solomon so illuminatingly as an obsessive desired master/bondsman relationship in Mozart's thought), something not at all present in Alfonso, who is not easily provoked, gives every appearance of wanting to play the game with his young friends, and seems completely untroubled by the pervasive faithlessness that his "scenes" have uncovered.

Alfonso, I believe, is an irreverent and later portrait of the senior patron, someone quite audaciously presented not as a moral instructor but as an amorous virtuoso, a libertine or retired rake whose influence is exerted through hoaxes, disguises, charades, and finally a philosophy of inconstancy as norm. Because he is an older and more resigned man, Alfonso intimates a sense of mortality that is very far from the concerns of the young lovers. A famous letter written by Wolfgang to Leopold in the final period of the latter's life (on April 4, 1787) expresses a mood of illusionless fatalism: "as death," Mozart says, "is the true goal of our existence, I have formed during the first few years such close relations with this best and truest friend of mankind, that his image is not only no longer terrifying to me, but is indeed very soothing and consoling! . . . death is *the* key which unlocks the door to our true happiness. I never lie down at night without reflecting that—young as I am—I may not live to see another day."[5] In the opera death is rendered less formidable and intimidating than it is for most people. This is not a conventionally Christian sentiment, however, but a naturalist one: death as something familiar and even dear, as a door to other experiences. Yet death is also represented as an inducement to a sense of fatalism and lateness—that is, the feeling that one is late in life, and the end is near.

So also in *Così fan tutte* the father figure has become the friend and cheerful, tyrannical mentor, a person to be obeyed who is somehow neither paternalistic nor minatory. And this status is confirmed in Mozart's style, in which posturing characters are displayed and presented in such a way as to permit Alfonso's ideas to enter into a game with them, not as a hectoring senior presence nor as an admonishing pedagogue but as an actor in the common entertainment. Alfonso predicts the conclusion or end of the comedy, but here, Donald Mitchell says,

> we stumble . . . on the most uncomfortable aspect of the opera's factuality. What we yearn for is the possibility of a fairy-tale reconciliation. But Mozart was far too truthful an artist to disguise the fact that a healing forgiveness is impossible where all the parties [Alfonso included] are not only equally "guilty" but share to the full the knowledge of each other's guilt. In *Così*, the best that can be done is to present as brave a front as one may to the fact of life [and, I could add, of death]. The coda that succeeds the *dénouement* does exactly that and no more.[6]

The conclusion of *Così* is really twofold: this is the way things are because that is what *they* do—*così fan tutte*—and second, they *will be* like that, one situation, one substitution succeeding another, until by implication the process is stopped by death. All are the same, *così fan tutte*, in the meantime. As Fiordiligi says, "*E potrà la morte sola far che cangi affetto il cor.*" Death takes the place of Christian reconciliation and redemption, the key to our *true,* if unknown and indescribable, hope of rest and stability, soothing and consoling without providing anything more than a theoretical intimation of final repose.

But like nearly every serious subject with which the opera flirts, death is kept at bay, indeed is mostly left out of *Così fan tutte.* Here we should recall those extraordinary feelings of solitary longing and coldness about which Mozart spoke while he worked on the opera. What affects us about *Così* is of course the music, which often seems so incongruously more interesting than the situation Mozart uses it for, except when (especially in the second act) the four lovers express their complex feelings of elation, regret, fear, and outrage. But even at such moments the disparity between Fiordiligi's assertion of faith and devotion in *"Come scoglio"* and the genuinely frivolous game she is involved in deflates the noble sentiments and music she utters, making that music seem both impossibly overstated and sensationally beautiful at the same time— a combination, I think, that corresponds to Mozart's feelings of unsatisfied longing and cold mastery. Listening to the aria and seeing the hubbub of serious and comic elements jostling one another on the stage, we are kept from wandering off into either speculation or despair, obligated to follow the tight discipline of Mozart's rigor.

I conclude by saying that within its carefully circumscribed limits, *Così fan tutte* allows itself only a number of gestures toward what stands just beyond it or, if I may vary the metaphor a bit, through what stands just inside it. Mozart never ventured closer to the potentially terrifying view he and Da Ponte seem to have uncovered of a universe shorn of any redemptive or palliative scheme, whose one law is motion and instability expressed as the power of libertinage and manipulation, and whose only conclusion is the terminal repose provided by death. That so astonishingly satisfying a musical score should be joined to so heedless and insignificant a tale is what *Così fan tutte* accomplishes with such unique virtuosity. But we should not, I think, believe that the candid fun of the work does any more than hold its ominous vision in abeyance—that is, for as long as *Così fan tutte*'s limits are not permitted to invade the stage.

FOUR

On Jean Genet

The first time I saw Jean Genet was in the spring of 1970, a the-
atrically turbulent and inchoate season when energies and
ambitions were released from the social imagination of America into its social body. There was always some excitement to
celebrate, some occasion to get up for, some new moment in
the Indochinese war either to lament or to demonstrate against.
Just a couple of weeks before the American invasion of Cam-
bodia, at what seemed the very height of the spring events at
Columbia University—which, it should be recalled, had still not
recovered from the upheavals of 1968: its administration was
feeling uncertain, its faculty were badly divided, its students
were perpetually exercised both in and out of the classroom—
a noon rally was announced in support of the Black Panthers.
It was to take place on the steps of Low Library, Columbia's
imposing administration building, and I was especially eager to
attend because the rumor was that Jean Genet was going to
speak. As I left Hamilton Hall for the rally, I met a student of
mine who had been particularly active on campus and who
assured me that Genet was indeed going to speak and that he,
the student, would be Genet's simultaneous interpreter.

It was an unforgettable scene for two reasons. One was the
deeply moving sight of Genet himself, who stood at the center

of a large crowd of Panthers and students—he was planted in the middle of the steps with his audience all around him rather than in front of him—dressed in his black leather jacket, blue shirt, and, I think, scruffy jeans. He seemed absolutely at rest, rather like the portrait of him by Giacometti, who caught the man's astounding combination of storminess, relentless control, and almost religious stillness. What I have never forgotten was the gaze of Genet's piercing blue eyes: they seemed to reach out across the distance and fix you with an enigmatic and curiously neutral look.

The other memorable aspect of that rally was the stark contrast between the declarative simplicity of Genet's French remarks in support of the Panthers and the immensely baroque embellishment of them by my erstwhile student. Genet would say, for example, "The Blacks are the most oppressed class in the United States." This would emerge in the translator's colorful ornamentation as something like "In this mother-fucking son-of-a-bitch country, in which reactionary capitalism oppresses and fucks over all the people, not just some of them, etc., etc." Genet stood through this appalling tirade unruffled, and even though the tables were sufficiently turned that the translator and not the speaker dominated the proceedings, the great writer never so much as blinked. This added to my respect and interest in the man, who was swept away without a flourish at the end of his all-too-brief comments. Having known Genet's literary achievements through teaching *Notre-Dame des Fleurs* and *The Thief's Journal*, I was surprised at what appeared from a distance to be his immaculate modesty, quite different from the violent and eccentric sentiments attributed to him by his translator, who allowed himself to ignore what Genet said during the rally in preference for the bordello and prison scatology of some of the plays and prose writings.

When I next saw Genet, it was in the late fall of 1972 in

Beirut, where I was spending a sabbatical year. An old school friend of mine, Hanna (John) Mikhail, had called me some time before and said that he would like to bring Genet around to meet me, but I hadn't taken the offer very seriously at first, partly because I couldn't imagine Hanna and Genet as friends, and partly because I still knew nothing about Genet's already considerable involvement with the Palestinian resistance movement.

In any event, Hanna Mikhail deserves to be remembered thirty years or so after the fact a little more substantially than I've just presented him. Hanna and I were exact contemporaries, he as a Palestinian undergraduate at Haverford in the mid-1950s, I at Princeton. We went to graduate school at Harvard at the same time, although he was in political science and Middle Eastern studies and I was in comparative literature and English. He was always an exceptionally decent, quiet, and intellectually brilliant man, who expressed to me a quite unique Palestinian Christian background, firmly rooted in the Quaker community of Ramallah. He was committed to Arab nationalism and, very much more than I, at home in both the Arab world and the West. I was flabbergasted when in 1969, after what I gathered was a difficult divorce from his American wife, he quit a good teaching position at the University of Washington and enlisted in the revolution, as we called it, which was headquartered in Amman. I met him there in 1969 and again in 1970 when, both before Black September and in its early days, he played a leading role as the head of information for Fateh.

Hanna's movement name was Abu Omar, and it is in that capacity and by that name that he appears in Genet's posthumous autobiographical work *Le captif amoureux* (the English title, *Prisoner of Love,* misses much that is subtly interesting in the French original), which I think Genet considered to be a continuation of *The Thief's Journal*. Published in 1986, *Le captif* is an astonishingly rich and rambling account of Genet's experiences with, feelings about, and reflections on the Palestinians, with whom he associated for about fifteen years. As I said, at the time of his visit I had no idea of Genet's already quite long involvement with the Palestinians; nor, in fact, did I know anything at all about his North African engagements, personal or political. Hanna had called at about eight that evening to say that they would both be dropping by a little later, and so after putting our infant son to bed, Mariam and I sat down to wait in the attractively warm and quiet Beirut evening.

I don't want to read too much into Genet's presence in that part of the world at that time, but it has seemed retrospectively to be a portent of much that has been bewildering and agonistically stunning about events in Jordan, Palestine, and Lebanon. The Lebanese Civil War would break out almost exactly three years later; Hanna would be killed four years later; the Israeli invasion of Lebanon would occur ten years later; *Le captif amoureux* would appear fourteen years later; and very important indeed from my point of view, the *intifada* that would lead to the declaration of a Palestinian state was to explode into actuality fifteen years later.

In the violence and incomprehensible beauty of the deeply shattering and disruptive events that have reconfigured an already absurdist landscape into an entirely new topography, it was Genet's quiet figure moving through the Levant that seemed to me, and doubtless to others, to have informed the dense fluidity of what would take place. I saw this largely because at the time I met him in 1972, even though I had not read or seen *Les paravents (The Screens)* and of course *Le captif amoureux* had not appeared, I sensed that this titanic artist and personality had intuited the scope and drama of what we were living through, in Lebanon, Palestine, and elsewhere. I could not have felt what I feel now, that the dislocating and yet rigorous energies and visions of *Les paravents* would not, could not, be stilled after Algerian independence in 1962 but would, like the nomadic figures spoken of by Gilles Deleuze and Felix Guattari in *Mille plateaux,* wander elsewhere in search of acknowledgment and illumination.

In manner and appearance he was as quiet and as modest as I had seen him at the time of the Columbia rally. He and Hanna appeared a little after ten and stayed till almost three in the morning. I don't think I could narrate the meandering discussions of that evening, but I do want to register a few impressions and anecdotes. Hanna remained fairly quiet throughout; he later told me that he had wanted to let me feel the full force of Genet's special vision of things without distraction, and hence his—Hanna's—relative withdrawal. Later I was able to read back into that gesture some of the forgiving permission that Hanna had given everyone around him, and how that permission to let people be themselves was the true focus of Hanna's search for liberation. Certainly it was clear that Genet appreciated this aspect of his companion's political mission; it was the deep bond between them, that both men in effect had united passion and an almost self-abnegating tolerance.

At the outset it seemed appropriate to tell Genet my spectator's side of the Panther rally, and to get his reaction to his interpreter's embellishments. He seemed unfazed by my student's ornaments: "I may not have said all those things," he said, "but," he added solemnly, *"je les pensais."* (I thought them.) We talked about Sartre, whose enormous tome on Genet, I suggested, must have made its subject slightly uneasy. Not at all, Genet replied unaffectedly, "if the guy wanted to make a saint of me, that's fine." In any case, he went on to say about Sartre's strong pro-Israeli position, "He's a bit of a coward for fear that his friends in Paris might accuse him of anti-Semitism if he ever said anything in support of Palestinian rights." Seven years later, when I was invited to a seminar in Paris about the Middle East organized by Simone de Beauvoir and Sartre, I remembered Genet's comment, struck by how this great Western intellectual whose work I had long admired was, so to speak, held in thrall to Zionism; this seemed totally to prevent him from saying a single word during the seminar about what the Palestinians had endured at the hands of Israel for so many decades. The proof of that is easily verified in the spring 1980 issue of *Les temps modernes,* which appeared with the full transcript of our seminar's desultory discussions a year earlier in Paris.

And so the conversation in Beirut went for hours, punctuated by what seemed to me to be Genet's long, puzzling, yet compellingly impressive silences. We spoke about his experiences in Jordan and Lebanon, his life and friends in France (toward which he expressed either deep hatred or total indifference). He smoked constantly, and he also drank, but he never seemed to change much either with drink, emotion, or thought. I recall that during the evening he once said something very positive and surprisingly warm about Jacques Derrida—*un copain,* remarked Genet—whom I had thought of as a quietist Heideggerian type at the time; *Glas* had not yet appeared, and it was only six months later, when Mariam, our little son, and I spent a few weeks in Paris, that I learned from Derrida himself that his friendship with Genet had originally been sealed as the two of them watched soccer matches together, which I thought was a nice touch. There is a brief allusion in *Glas* to our little encounter at Reid Hall in April 1973, although I've always been slightly miffed that Derrida should refer to me anonymously only as *"un ami"* who brought him news of Genet.

But to return to Genet in Beirut: the overwhelming impression he made on me was, I recollect, that he seemed totally unlike anything of his that I had read. And I then understood how on a number of occasions, most notably in one of the letters on *Les paravents* to Roger Blin, he says in fact that everything he wrote was written *"contre moi-même,"* a motif that turns up again in his 1977 interview with Hubert Fichte, where he says that only when he is alone does he tell the truth, a notion elaborated somewhat in his interview with *La revue d'études palestiniennes*, in 1983, that *"dès que je parle je suis trahi par la situation. Je suis trahi par celui qui m'écoute, tout simplement à cause de la communication. Je suis trahi par le choix de mes mots."*[1] (as soon as I speak I am betrayed by the situation. I am betrayed by the person who is listening to me, quite simply because I am speaking. I am betrayed by the choice of words.) These comments helped me to interpret his disconcertingly long silences, particularly at a time when, in his visits with the Palestinians, he was quite consciously acting in support of people for whom he cared, and for whom, he says in the Fichte interview, he felt an erotic attraction.

Still, with Genet's work, in contrast to that of any other major writer, you feel that his words, the situations he describes, and the characters he depicts—no matter how intensely, no matter how forcefully—are provisional. It is always the propulsive force driving him and his characters that Genet's work delivers most accurately, not the correctness or the content of what is said, or how the characters think or feel. His later works—most notably *Les paravents* and *Le captif amoureux*—are quite explicit, indeed scandalous, in this regard. Much more important than commitment to a cause, much more beautiful and true, he says, is betraying it, which I read as another version of his unceasing search for the silence that reduces all language to empty posturing, all action to theatrics. And yet Genet's essentially antithetical mode oughtn't to be

denied, either. He was in fact in love with the Arabs he drew in
Les paravents and in *Le captif amoureux,* the truth of which
does shine through the explicit denials and negations.

Is this a kind of overturned or exploded Orientalism? For
not only did Genet allow his love for them to be his approach
to the Arabs, he seems not to have aspired to a special position
(like some benevolent White Father) when he was with them or
writing about them. On the other hand, one never felt that he
tried to go native, be someone other than he was. There is no
evidence at all that he relied on colonial knowledge or lore to
guide him, and he did not resort, in what he wrote or said, to
clichés about Arab customs, or mentality, or tribal past, which
he might have used to interpret what he saw or felt. However
he might initially have made his first contacts with the Arabs
(*Le captif* suggests that he first fell in love with an Arab while
an eighteen-year-old soldier in Damascus half a century ago)
he entered the Arab space and lived in it not as an investiga-
tor of exoticism but as someone for whom the Arabs had actuality and a present that he enjoyed and felt comfortable in,
even though he was, and remained, different. In the context of
a dominant Orientalism that commanded, codified, and articulated virtually all Western knowledge and experience of the
Arab/Islamic world, there is something quietly but heroically
subversive about Genet's extraordinary relationship with the
Arabs.

These matters lay a special kind of obligation on Arab readers and critics of Genet, which compels us to read him with
unusual attention. Yes, he was a lover of Arabs—something
not many of us are accustomed to from Western writers and
thinkers, who have found an adversarial relationship with us
more congenial—and it is this particular emotion that stamps
his last major works. Both were written as frankly partisan
works, *Les paravents* in support of Algerian resistance during

the height of the colonial struggle, *Le captif* in support of Palestinian resistance from the late 1960s until his death in 1986, so that one is left in no doubt where Genet stood. His anger and enmity against France had autobiographical roots; on one level therefore to attack France in *Les paravents* was for him to transgress against the government that had judged and confined him to places like La Mettray. But on another level France represents the authority into which all social movements normally harden once they have achieved success. Genet celebrates Said's* betrayal in *Les paravents* not only because it guarantees the prerogative of freedom and beauty for an individual in perpetual revolt but also because, by its preemptive violence, it is a way of forestalling what revolutions in course never admit: that their first great enemies—and victims—after they triumph are likely to be the artists and intellectuals who supported the revolution for love and not because of the accidents of nationality, or the likelihood of success, or the dictates of theory.

Genet's attachment to Palestine was intermittent. After some years of abatement it was revived in the fall of 1982, which was when he returned to Beirut and wrote his memorable piece on the Sabra and Shatila massacres. He made clear, however, that what tied him to Palestine (he says this in the concluding pages of *Le captif*) *after* revolution was forgotten in Algeria was that it continued in the Palestinian struggle. Precisely what was obdurate, defiant, and radically transgressive in Said's gestures, as well as in the life-after-death speeches of the Mother, Leila, and Khadija in *Les paravents,* can be thought of as surviving from the play and is carried over into Palestinian resistance. Yet in that last great prose work of his one can see Genet's self-absorption struggling with his self-forgetfulness

*the protagonist

while his Western-French-Christian identity grapples with an entirely different and other culture. And it is in this encounter that Genet's exemplary greatness comes forward and in an almost Proustian way retrospectively illuminates *Les paravents*.

For the greatness of the play, in all its lurid, unremitting, and often comic theatricality, is its deliberate and logical dismantling not just of French identity—France as empire, as power, as history—but of the very notion of identity itself. Both the nationalism in whose name France subjugated Algeria, and the nationalism in whose name the Algerians resisted France since 1830, rely to a very great extent upon a politics of identity. As Genet said to Roger Blin, it was all one big event, from Dey's *coup d'eventail* in 1830 to the massive support of 800,000 *pieds noirs* for Tixier-Vignancour, the extreme-right-wing French lawyer who defended General Raoul Salan in the trials of 1962. France, France, France, as in the slogan *Algérie française*. But the opposite and equal reaction of the Algerians was also an affirmation of identity, by which the affiliation between combatants, the suffusing presence of patriotism, even the justified violence of the oppressed to which Genet always gave his unequivocal support, were all mobilized in the single-minded cause of *Algérie pour les algériens*. The gesture that contains the extreme radicality of Genet's anti-identitarian logic is of course Said's betrayal of his comrades, and the various incantations to evil pronounced by the women. It is also to be found in the intended décor, costumes, and verbal as well as gestural impropriety that gives the play its terrible force. *Pas de joliesse,* said Genet to Blin, for if there was one thing the negative force of the play could not tolerate, it was prettification, or palliation, or any sort of inconstancy to its rigor.

We are closer to Genet's solitary truth, as opposed to his sense of compromise whenever language is used, when we take seriously therefore his description of the play as a *poetic defla-*

gration, an artificially started and hastened chemical fire whose purpose is to light up the landscape as it turns all identities into combustible things like Sir Harold's rosebushes, which are set aflame by the Algerians in *Les paravents,* even as he prates on unheedingly. This notion also explains Genet's various, often very modestly and tentatively expressed requests that the play not be performed too many times. Genet was too serious a mind to assume that audiences, or actors and directors for that matter, could live through the apocalyptic purifications of the loss of identity on a daily basis. *Les paravents* has to be experienced as something altogether rare.

No less uncompromising is *Le captif amoureux.* There is no narrative in it, no sequential or thematically organized reflection on politics, love, or history. Indeed, one of the book's most remarkable accomplishments is that it somehow pulls one along uncomplainingly, in its meandering, often startlingly abrupt shifts of mood and logic. To read Genet is in the end to accept the utterly undomesticated peculiarity of his sensibility, which returns constantly to that area where revolt, passion, death, and regeneration are linked:

What was to become of you after the storms of fire and steel? What were you to do? Burn, shriek, turn into a brand, blackness. Turn to ashes, let yourself be slowly covered first with dust and then with earth, seeds, moss, leaving behind nothing but your jawbone and teeth, and finally becoming a little funeral mound with flowers growing on it and nothing inside.[2]

In their movement of regenerative rebellion, the Palestinians, like the Algerians and Black Panthers before them, show Genet a new language, not of orderly communication, but of astonishing lyricism, of a prelogical and yet highly wrought intensity that delivers "moments of wonder and . . . flashes of comprehension." Many of the most memorable fragments in the mysteriously digressive structure of *Le captif amoureux* meditate on language, which Genet always wants to transform from a force for identity and statement into a transgressive, disruptive, and perhaps even consciously evil mode of betrayal. "Once we see in the need to 'translate' the obvious need to 'betray,' we shall see the temptation to betray as something desirable, comparable perhaps to erotic exaltation. Anyone who hasn't experienced the ecstasy of betrayal knows nothing about ecstasy at all" (LCA 85/59). There is in this admission the very same dark force of the Mother, Khadija, Leila, and Said in *Les paravents*, partisans of Algerian liberation who nevertheless exultantly betray their comrades.

The challenge of Genet's writing therefore is its fierce anti-nomianism. Here is a man in love with "the other," an outcast and stranger himself, feeling the deepest sympathy for the Palestinian revolution as the "metaphysical" uprising of out-casts and strangers—"my heart was in it, my body was in it; my spirit was in it"—yet neither his "total belief," nor "the whole of myself" could be in it (LCA 125/90). The conscious-ness of being a sham, an unstable personality perpetually at the border ("where human personality expresses itself most fully, whether in harmony or in contradiction with itself" [LCA 203/147]) is the central experience of the book. "My whole life was made up of unimportant trifles cleverly blown up into acts of daring" (LCA 205/148). One is immediately reminded here of T. E. Lawrence, an imperial agent among the Arabs (though pretending to be otherwise) half a century earlier, but Lawrence's assertiveness and instinct for detached domination are superseded in Genet (who was no agent) by eroticism and an authentic submission to the political sweep of a passionate commitment.

Identity is what we impose on ourselves through our lives as social, historical, political, and even spiritual beings. The logic of culture and of families doubles the strength of identity, which to someone like Genet who was a victim of the identity forced on him by his delinquency, his isolation, and his transgressive talents and delights—is something to be resolutely opposed. Above all, given Genet's choice of sites like Algeria and Palestine, identity is the process by which the stronger culture, and the more developed society, imposes itself violently upon those who, by the same identity process, are decreed to be a lesser people. Imperialism is the export of identity.

Genet therefore is the traveler across identities, the tourist whose purpose is marriage with a foreign cause, so long as that cause is both revolutionary and in constant agitation. Despite their prohibitions, he says in *Le captif*, frontiers are fascinating because a Jacobin who crosses frontiers must change into a Machiavellian. The revolutionary, in other words, will occasionally accommodate himself to the customs post, haggling, brandishing a passport, applying for visas, humbling himself before the State. Genet never did this, so far as I can tell: in Beirut he spoke to us with rare joviality of how he entered the United States from Canada, surreptitiously and illegally. The choice of Algeria and Palestine was not exoticism, however, but a dangerous and subversive politics involving borders that had to be negotiated, expectations to be fulfilled, dangers to be dealt with. And to speak here as a Palestinian, I believe that Genet's choice of Palestine in the 1970s and 1980s was the most dangerous political choice, the scariest journey of all. Only Palestine has not been coopted in the West either by the dominant liberal or the dominant establishment political culture. Ask any Palestinian, and he or she will tell you how our identity is still the only criminalized and delinquent selfhood, whose Western codeword is *terrorism*, in a historical period in the West that has empowered, liberated, or variously dignified most other races and nationalities. So the choice first of Algeria in the 1950s, then of Palestine in the period thereafter, is and ought to be understood as a vital act of Genet's solidarity, his willing enraptured identification with other identities whose existence involves a strenuously contested struggle.

So identity grates against identity, and the dissolution of identity undermines both. Genet is thus the most antithetical of imaginations. Ruling all of his endeavors is rigor and elegance, embodied in what Richard Howard has called one of the greatest formal French styles since Chateaubriand. One never feels any sort of sloppiness or diversion in what he does, any more than one would expect Genet to have worn a three-piece suit to go to work in an office. His nomadic energies are housed in linguistic precision and grace, albeit in trajectories without romantic hope or routinized discomfort. Genius *(le génie)*, he once said, *"c'est la rigueur dans le désespoir."* How perfectly that sense is caught in Khadija's great ode to *"le mal"* in scene 12 of *Les paravents,* in its combination of hieratic severity and its surprising self-deflation, all contained in a rhythm of high formality that suggests an unlikely combination of Racine and Zazie.[3]

Genet is like that other great modern dissolver of identity, Adorno, for whom no thought is translatable into any other equivalent, yet whose relentless urge to communicate his precision and desperation—with the fineness and counternarratival energy that makes *Minima Moralia* his masterpiece—furnishes a perfect metaphysical accompaniment to Genet's funeral pomp and his scabrous raucousness. What we miss in Adorno is Genet's scurrilous humor, so evident in his booming send-ups of Sir Harold and his son, the vamps and missionaries, whores and French soldiers of *Les paravents.*

Adorno, however, is a minimalist whose distrust and hatred

of the totality caused him to work entirely in fragments, aphorisms, essays, and digressions. As opposed to Adorno's micrologics, Genet is a poet of large dionysiac forms, of ceremonies and carnivalesque display: his work is related to the Ibsen of *Peer Gynt,* to the theater of Artaud, Peter Weiss, and Aime Césaire. His characters interest us not because of their psychology but because in their own obsessive ways they are the paradoxically causal and yet formalistic bearers of a very finely imagined and understood history. Genet made the step, crossed the legal borders, that very few white men or women even attempted. He traversed the space from the metropolitan center to the colony; his unquestioned solidarity was with the very same oppressed identified and so passionately analyzed by Fanon. His characters therefore are play-actors in a history imposed on them by power—the power of the imperial state as well as the power of the insurrectionary natives.

I don't think it is wrong to say that in the twentieth century with very few exceptions great art in a colonial situation always appears in support of what Genet in *Le captif* calls the metaphysical uprising of the natives. The cause of Algeria produced *Les paravents,* Pontecorvo's *Battle of Algiers,* Fanon's books, the works of Kateb Yacine. Compared to these works, Camus pales, his novels, essays, and stories the desperate gestures of a frightened, finally ungenerous mind. In Palestine the same is true, since the radical, transformative, difficult, and visionary work comes from and on behalf of the Palestinians— Habibi, Darwish, Jabra, Kanafani, Tuqan, Kassem, Genet— not from the Israelis, who oppose them for the most part. Genet's works are, to borrow a phrase from Raymond Williams, resources of hope. In 1961 he could complete an overwhelmingly theatrical work like *Les paravents* because, I believe, victory for the FLN was very near at hand: the play catches the moral exhaustion of France and the moral triumph of the FLN.

When it came to Palestine, however, Genet found the Palestinians in an apparently uncertain phase, with the disasters of Jordan and Lebanon recently behind them and the dangers of more dispossession, exile, and dispersion all around them. Hence, as I said above, the ruminative, exploratory, and intimate quality of *Le captif amoureux*—anti-theatrical, radically contradictory, rich in memory and speculation.

> This is *my* Palestinian revolution, told in my *own* chosen order. As well as mine there is the other, probably many others.
>
> Trying to think the revolution is like waking up and trying to see the logic in a dream. There's no point, in the middle of a drought, in imagining how to cross the river when the bridge has been swept away. When, half awake, I think about the revolution, I see it as the tail of a caged tiger, starting to lash out in a vast sweep, then falling back wearily on the prisoner's flank. (LCA 416/309)

One would have wished Genet alive today for many reasons, not least because of the Palestinian uprising, the *intifada,* on the West Bank and Gaza, which began in 1987. It is not farfetched to say that *Les paravents* is Genet's version of an Algerian *intifada,* given flesh and blood in the beauty and exuberance of the Palestinian *intifada.* Life imitates art, but so also does art—in the extraordinary November 1989 Guthrie Theater production of *Les paravents* directed by Joanne Akalaitis—imitate life and, insofar as it can be imitated, death.

Genet's last works are saturated with images of death, especially *Le captif,* part of whose melancholy for the reader is the knowledge that Genet was dying as he wrote the book, and that so many of the Palestinians he saw, knew, and wrote about were also to die. It is curious, however, that both *Le captif* and

Les paravents end with affirmative recollections of a mother
and her son who, although dead or about to die, are reunited
by Genet in his own mind; the act of reconciliation and apparent recollection that occurs at the end of *Les paravents,* as
Said and the Mother are seen together, prefigures Genet's last
prose work by twenty-five years. These are firmly unsentimen-
tal scenes, partly because Genet seems determined to present
death as a weightless and largely unchallenging thing. Genet
also wants to retain for his own purposes the priority and affective comfort of the relationship between an almost savagely
archetypal Mother (who is not named but referred to simply as
"la mère" in both books) and a loyal but somewhat aloof,
often harsh Son. Aside from the perfectly obvious absence of a
threateningly authoritative Father, Genet's imagination articu-
lates an unarguably final moment in what are for him trans-
posed terms: both mother-son pairs are people he likes and
admires, but neither in the play nor in the memoir are he and
his mother present.

That he is involved in the scene, however, is unmistakable,
especially in *Le captif* since his experiences with the maternally
defined pair (Hamza and his mother) are specifically recalled.
A primordial relationship—fierce, loving, enduring—is therefore imagined as persisting beyond death. Yet so meticulous is
Genet's refusal to concede that any good can come from per-
manence or from bourgeois (and heterosexual) stability that he
dissolves even these positive images of death in the ceaseless
social turbulence and revolutionary disruption that are central
to his interest. Yet it is the mother in both works who is
strangely unyielding, uncompromising, difficult. *"Tu ne vas
pas flancher,"* his mother reminds Said, you are *not* to be
coopted; and you are not to become a domesticated symbol
or a martyr for the revolution. When Said finally disappears at
the end of the play (undoubtedly killed), it is once again the

mother who with considerable anxiety and, I think, disgust suggests that Said *might* be forced by his comrades to come back in a commemorative revolutionary song.

Genet does not want the death that awaits and will surely claim him and his characters to invade, arrest, or seriously modify any aspect of the rushing turmoil that his work represents as deflagration, which he imagines to be centrally, even mystically important. It is startling to find this irreducibly religious conviction so close to his heart at the end. For whether demon or divinity, the Absolute for Genet is perceptible neither in the form of human identity nor as a personified deity but precisely in what after everything is said and done will not settle down, will not be incorporated or domesticated. That such a force must somehow be represented and cared for by people who are absorbed in it and, at the same time, that it must risk its own disclosure or personification is Genet's final, most intransigent paradox. Even when we close the book or leave the theater once the performance is over, his work instructs us also to block the song, doubt the narrative and memory, disregard the aesthetic experience that brought us those images for which we now have a genuinely strong affection. That so impersonal and true a philosophical dignity should also be allied with so poignantly human a sensibility is what gives Genet's work the unreconciled and tense note it communicates. In no other late-twentieth-century writer are the grand dangers of catastrophe and the lyrical delicacy of affective response to them sustained together as grandly and fearlessly.

FIVE

A Lingering Old Order

Adorno speaks of Beethoven's late works as constitutively alienated and alienating: difficult, forbidding works like the *Missa Solemnis* and the *Hammerklavier* Sonata are repellent to audiences and performers alike both because of their redoubtable technical challenges and because their disjointed, even distracted sense of internal continuity offers no very easy line to follow. Adorno argues that whereas Bach could approach fugue subjects with a kind of direct, fresh naïveté similar to the relationship between "subjective" composers and their *cantabile*-like inspirations, in the *Missa Solemnis* there "disappeared a harmony of the musical subject and the musical forms which had permitted something akin to naïveté in Schiller's sense of the word. The objectivity of the musical forms with which Beethoven worked in the *Missa* is mediated and problematic—an object of reflection."[1] As for the religious element in the *Missa,* here Adorno ventures the daring thesis that like Kant, Beethoven was posing the question of ultimate ontology in terms of subjectivity, and practically the work asks the question of "what and how one may sing of the absolute without deceit." Adorno consequently offers a stunningly imaginative analysis of the *Missa*'s stylization and archaisms, its movement backward "toward something unexpressed, undefined," with a result in scholastic stylization and indirection based on compositional fantasy that give the work its strangely inconclusive, mystifying quality. Bereft of ultimate harmony between subjective and objective—here Adorno reasserts the primacy in the late Beethoven of an irreconcilable, permanently unresolved internal opposition—the *Missa* in reality "is a work of . . . exclusion, of permanent renunciation." What it also renounces in the process is the aim of reconciling "the universally human" with a concrete way of being human. This somewhat disenchanted realization on Beethoven's part is what Adorno calls with some irony "an effort of the later bourgeois spirit."[2]

Adorno exemplifies the European intellectual who refused to compromise with the culture industry as he saw it. His characteristic anti-identitarian notion is that of antinomian opposition, unresolved contradictions that he believed he existed to maintain, insist on, and gloss in a prose that—whether in German or in the various translations that have been made of it—remains permanently, fanatically difficult. As I also said, Adorno is lateness itself, hell-bent on remaining untimely and contrary in the Nietzschean sense.

But you could pull off such a patently unattractive style if you were as genuinely clever as Adorno and if your métier was writing about Berg, Beethoven, Husserl, and Hegel. Adorno was principally an essayist, and the essay was the form that he said "is concerned with what is blind in its objects" and whose "innermost formal law is heresy." To be an essayist in Adorno's sense meant to be permanently on strike from, and at odds with, everything fashionable, à la mode, *in,* intellectually speaking. Typically, he added, "the contemporary relevance of the essay is that of anachronism."[3] Richard Strauss was equally anachronistic—a composer of classical music in an age when that inevitably meant not being part of the gigantic network of producers and consumers whose major experience might have been Walt Disney's *Fantasia* or performances by José Iturbi and Oscar Levant in the tonier Hollywood musicals. For all his geniality Strauss too was a late-style exponent in his last works, retreating into an elusive mix of eighteenth-century instrumentation and deceptively simple and rarified chamber expression designed to outrage his avant-garde contemporaries as much as his local and by-now-uninteresting audiences. Yet Strauss and Adorno belong essentially to a high-culture enclave shielded somewhat from the rigors and demands and, yes, rewards of Hollywood films and mass-market novels. How then does late style manifest itself in those altogether more accessible realms?

A remarkable coincidence of talents in Italy between 1958, when Lampedusa's *Il gattopardo* was posthumously published, and 1963, when Luchino Visconti's film of the novel appeared, provides us with a wonderful opportunity to explore the matter. It is an infrequent occurrence, this fusion of two aristocratic and deeply anachronistic gifts with a big publishing success and an equally big film success.

The Sicilian aristocrat Giuseppe Tomasi di Lampedusa (1896–1957) did not begin work on *The Leopard* until late in life. He was fearful perhaps of a bad reception on the mainland and also unwilling to compete with other writers. He was steeped in Italian literature and culture, but unlike many of his contemporaries he was also a serious, even scholarly expert on French (especially medieval and Renaissance) and, more unusually, English literature. His English biographer David Gilmour describes in detail how Lampedusa instructed his nephew and a small number of young men in the study of literature, taking them painstakingly into the earlier classics through to nineteenth-century fiction (his favorite was Stendhal) and on into the twentieth century. By the end of 1954, saturated in the contemplation of other works, he began his own novel. Gilmour guesses that Lampedusa was moved to write by his sense that as an "ultimate descendant of an ancient noble line whose economic and physical extinction culminated in himself," he would be the last member of his family to have "vital memories" or to be capable of evoking a "unique Sicilian world" before it disappeared.[4] He was interested in (and depressed by) the process of decadence, one sign of which was the loss of family property—a house in Santa Margherita (Donnafugata in the novel) and a palace in Palermo.

Lampedusa's only novel, *The Leopard* was turned down by many publishers before Feltrinelli made an almost instant bestseller of it in November 1958, a year after its author's death. Four years later Luchino Visconti began and completed filming of the novel; the film was first shown in March 1963, although for various commercial reasons it was for a long time virtually impossible to see the original 185-minute version. Burt Lancaster portrays the Prince of Salina, Claudia Cardinale is Angelica, Alain Delon is Tancredi. Although it was preceded in Visconti's oeuvre by *Senso,* a historical costume drama, *The Leopard*—in its sumptuous and even lavish theatricality, its spectacularly realistic and resplendent interiors, its larger-than-life, almost allegorical figures—inaugurated the final phase of its director's career. After *The Leopard* came *Death in Venice, The Damned, Ludwig, The Stranger,* and *The Innocent,* most of them large historical films redolent of the operatic world, in which Visconti was also very active. He died in 1976, leaving unfinished his plans to produce a *Ring* cycle at La Scala, as well as a film of Proust's great novel. All of his late-period work therefore concentrates on themes having to do with degeneration, the passing of an old and generally aristocratic order, the unpleasant emergence of a new and crass middle-class world, represented in *The Leopard* by Don Calogero, the wealthy and crude but effective parvenu whose daughter marries into the old Sicilian aristocracy.

Both Lampedusa and Visconti were themselves aristocrats, representatives of the very order whose demise their works present. Yet both of them worked through genres—the novel and the feature film—that have a complicated mass-society history that is mostly at odds with the story that Lampedusa tells and that Visconti's film adapts and reenacts on the big screen. It is worth noting that Visconti not only was a Marxist but began his career as a filmmaker by producing a series of films (such as *La terra trema*) that were solidly, even conventionally, within the neorealist tradition of Rossellini and the early De Sica. Unlike his younger contemporary Gillo Pontecorvo, who also began work in the wave created by Rossellini, Visconti continued his career outside that wave, although he remained a Marxist. (His biographer Laurence Schifano reports that after finishing *The Leopard,* Visconti delayed his next film *Vaghe stelle dell'orsa*—also known as *Sandra*—"because of the death of the Communist Party leader Palmiro Togliatti," at whose coffin Visconti kept vigil.)[5] Pontecorvo made *The Battle of Algiers* at roughly the time *The Leopard* was being filmed; a few years later *Burn!* followed, just as *The Damned (La caduta degli dei)* was being shot. But whereas Pontecorvo evolved out of neorealism into a brilliantly invented, quasi-documentary revolutionary, even agitational style that he transported out of Italy to a third-world colonial war, Visconti retreated back into a more sophisticated and refined version of an older form, the grand historical epic associated with Hollywood films of the 1940s and 1950s, using as his subject matter a sort of nostalgia for an old class that is threatened by the depredations of both popular revolution and the new bourgeois order. Early socialist interpretations of the film accused Visconti at the time of historical and political quietism, a charge that has stuck to the film and is one of the reasons it was so hard to find.

Superficially, Lampedusa's novel is not an experimental work. Its major technical innovation is that the narrative is composed discontinuously, as a series of relatively discrete but highly wrought fragments or episodes, each organized around a date and in some instances an event, as in the sixth chapter, "A Ball: November 1862," which becomes perhaps the most famous and certainly the longest and most complex sequence in Visconti's film. This technique allowed Lampedusa a measure of freedom from the exigencies of the plot, which is almost primitive, freeing him to work instead with the memories and future occasions (for example, the Allied landing in 1944) that radiate from the simple events of the narrative.

The Leopard is the story of the elderly Sicilian Prince of Salina, Don Fabrizio, a giant of a man whose estates are crumbling and who now feels the approach of death. A great astronomer, he spends his time tending a wife, three unsatisfactory daughters, and two average sons. His dashing nephew Tancredi is his only pleasure. Tancredi has fallen in love with Angelica, the beautiful daughter of a merchant parvenu. The story unfolds during Garibaldi's campaign to unify Italy, a period that marks the final decline of the old aristocratic order, of whom the prince is the last and noblest representative. When Don Calogero visits the prince to receive an offer of marriage for his daughter Angelica, the exchange between the two men is marvelously inflated with Fabrizio's observations, his dress and toilet, and his reflections on the future. Calogero meanwhile is given a chance to embroider his own past, so that before the reader's eyes the unattractive provincial entrepre-

neur can be seen inventing a family tradition for himself (he
tells the prince that his daughter Angelica is really Baronessina
Sedàra del Biscotto) and at the same time buying off the
prince's dashing young nephew. Lampedusa then considers
Tancredi's brilliant future and the further decline of the Salina
fortune, and in a sort of afterthought, he allows the prince to
be reminded of his poor retainer, Don Ciccio, whom he had
locked up in a gun room to safeguard the secret of the Tancredi
proposal until the deal was concluded. Little details abound.
After he has described both the misfortunes and the excellence
of Tancredi and his family, he says with a princely flourish:
"The result of all these disasters . . . has been Tancredi. There
are certain things known to people like us; and maybe it is
impossible to obtain the distinction, the delicacy, the fascina-
tion of a boy like him without his ancestors having romped
through half a dozen fortunes." Such passages give the episodes
their metaphoric and literal richness, and it is this that the novel
as a whole communicates: a world of great, even luxurious, but
now inaccessible privilege connected with, or more accurately
giving rise to, that particular melancholy associated with senescence, loss, and death. Gilmour speaks of Lampedusa's classifi-
cation of writers into the categories of *magri, super magri,* and
grassi: in the first were Laclos, Calvin, Madame de Lafayette,
in the second La Rochefoucauld and Mallarmé, and in the third
Dante, Rabelais, Shakespeare, Balzac, and Proust. Lampedusa's
own novel seemed to be a *magro* in the spareness and unfussi-
ness of its style, but its detail and suggestion are in the *grassi*
category.[6]

The point is that Lampedusa's novel is of a popular genre
that might today be known as "secrets of the rich and famous"
were it not also influenced by two powerful cultural antecedents, who mean a great deal to Visconti as well: Proust and
Gramsci. The affinities between the two twentieth-century Ital-

ians and Proust are numerous. Like him, they redeem a popular form for a brooding yet generally accessible meditation on the passing of time seen from the perspective of society—that is, worldliness, savoir-faire, aristocratic grace, and a certain superfluity. Proust was one of Lampedusa's favorite authors partly, I think, because both men shared that feeling of an immobilized present animated and enlarged by a sustained reflection on the past. The Prince of Salina's large size and the impression given of him by the novel of stretching back in time, immersed in time like a giant in water, is very Proustian. And the sense of all-pervading mortality that envelops the action of *The Leopard* suggests the very late passages of *À la recherche*, in particular Marcel's return to Paris, now strikingly decayed after World War I, although unlike Proust, Lampedusa provides no theory of redemptive art at the end. Unlike Proust as well, Lampedusa is neither a snob nor a gossip but is a real aristocrat who spends very little time anatomizing the affairs, malice, and infinitely complicated hurts administered to one another by various members of his cast. Sicily in the 1860s was not Paris, after all, and no one in the novel is in effect a great deal more than a provincial. In any event, Proust and Lampedusa both share a pronounced affection for the aristocracy, whose weakened and diminished status represents to them the regretted end of an era.

Laurence Schifano quotes Visconti in 1971 saying that because he was born in 1906, he "belonged to the period of Mann, Proust and Mahler."[7] No one who has read anything about Visconti's background and upbringing can fail to be impressed by the similarity between his world and the world of aristocracy described so memorably by Proust. Like Proust, he was exceptionally close to his beautiful and gifted mother; and like Proust, he was homosexual. If Lampedusa's is a world of political and economic decadence, Visconti's is closer to

Proust's; it is morally and spiritually corrupt, yet enormously compelling despite its almost unimaginable sordidness. There is a puzzling break in aesthetic continuity here: Visconti's early films through *Rocco and His Brothers* are exercises in discipline; they are ascetic, realistic, spare, and controlled. From *The Leopard* on, it is as if he let himself go in the films, and they achieve a kind of lushness that contrasts very interestingly with his earlier work. And although in an interview published with the script of *The Leopard* Visconti claims to have chosen Proust over Verga (the filter of memory over the direct and realistic record of actual events), most critics see in Visconti's film—in particular the last sequence, that of the enormous ball scene—a lapse into uncritical nostalgia, very different from the astringent dedication to art of Marcel. Visconti is said to have thought of Tancredi and Angelica as Swann and Odette. We recall that in *À la recherche* the narrator self-consciously sets about the task of re-creating lost time, thus completely identifying the artistic vocation with memory. However, as Geoffrey Nowell-Smith puts it in his excellent book about Visconti,

the pomp and splendor of the aristocratic ball and the patriarchal figure of Burt Lancaster as the Prince appear almost to have taken precedence over the themes developed earlier in the film, and gradually edged them out to allow for the virtual transfiguration of the Sicilian aristocracy in the tremendous finale. Not only has the episode grown in physical size, so that contrary to original indications it now lasts, in its complete form, for well over an hour; it has also acquired a character of unquestioning nostalgia. Where the film had previously taken a critical attitude to the events described, it now slides gently into sharing the point of view of one of the protagonists. Given the manner in which the Prince has been idealized as a figure right from the beginning, the move into *style indirect*

libre can be interpreted in only one way, as identification by
Visconti with the central figure.[8]

Nowell-Smith's analyses here amount to a characterization
of what less charitable critics have referred to as Viscontian
narcissism. This theme is developed by Bernard Dort in a tough-
minded article for *Les temps modernes* in 1963, in which he
identifies Visconti's *Leopard* not with the Proust of *À la
recherche* but with the earlier, self-indulgent, and soft melancholy of *Les plaisirs et les jours*. I think it is more correct to
say that Visconti imbibed a generally Proustian atmosphere to
some extent from his own predilections and background but
more importantly from Lampedusa himself. Except for the last
two chapters, Visconti's screenplay follows the novel with
meticulous fidelity, especially when it comes to keeping the
prince at the center of consciousness and of the action. Visconti
eliminates the last chapters of the novel entirely and nowhere
shows us the prince in his final illness and death.

There the prince lies in a shabby Palermo hotel, exhausted
by his trip back from Naples, where he has gone to see a spe-
cialist. Concetta and Francesco Paolo, his oldest daughter and
youngest son, are with him, as is his beloved Tancredi. It is July
1883: the prince is seventy-three. Nothing in what transpires
carries the slightest hint of redemption, or of an artistic vocation of the kind that lifts Marcel from the level of the lazy ren-
tier to that of committed writer. Don Fabrizio is filled with a
consciousness of being the last Salina: "he was alone, a ship-
wrecked man adrift on a raft, prey of untameable currents."
All he has left is a train of memories, but they too are under-
mined by his sense of being the last person to have them. The
only qualification of this gloomy picture is the prince's scientific interest in nature, the stars particularly, which draws him
briefly out of his dying agony and submits him to the rhythms

of the all-encompassing ocean, whose emissary, in a final touch of genius, seems to be the beautiful but now unnamed Angelica, who has become a type of generalized feminine sensuality. Her unexpected and sudden presence at his bedside seems to unlock his repressed passion for her, and that in turn delivers him to his natural end.

I'd like to return to these transformations of Proust in a moment, but I must first say something about the second presiding mind, Gramsci's, in both film and novel. Gramsci's last uncompleted work before he was imprisoned by Mussolini in 1926 was *La questione meridionale (The Southern Question)*, a longish draft of which survives and that constitutes the single most concentrated and sustained piece of writing that Gramsci ever attempted. Its importance as a work whose thought and influence in many ways prepared the ground for Lampedusa and Visconti is profound. As a Sardinian, Gramsci understood the South—its poverty, its underdevelopment, its exploitation by the North—from personal experience. But what is impressive about Gramsci's analyses of the Southern Question is that he situates the problem within the structure of Italian history since (but also before) the Risorgimento. What the unification of Italy did to places like Sicily, Naples, and Sardinia was to arrest and distort, then to isolate them in their lopsided social, economic, and certainly political actualities. To Gramsci, then, the South appears, he says memorably, like a vast social disintegration: a large mass of destitute and oppressed peasants are preyed on by a class of parasitic intermediaries (priests, teachers, tax collectors) on behalf of a small group of great landowners. With unusual insight Gramsci shows how the presence as well of large publishing houses (Laterza, for example) and massive cultural figures (the greatest of whom is Benedetto Croce) exist alongside, and curiously unconnected to, the crumbling, indeed worsening economic situation of the peasantry.

Add to this the way even the emerging working-class movement of the North—the factory workers, organizers, and intellectuals around Turin and Milan—has treated the South, leaving it unincluded in the project of Italian unity begun by the Risorgimento, and Gramsci says, you have an appalling problem.

For Gramsci, the South is of course an actual place, but as he talks about some of the peculiarities of Italian society in his prison notes, one begins to understand that for him the South symbolized two things more. One was a society dominated as an inferior, frozen in a state of permanent binarism, by a stronger outside partner. Two was an uncompleted social elaboration, a residue from the days before unification, a static part of the whole of Italy that had to be animated and invigorated organically. Gramsci's analysis of the Southern Question is enclosed within his broader considerations of Italian history, given complex albeit lapidary treatment in the prison notebooks and collected under the title "Notes on Italian History." Much of what he has to say here directly concerns the subject of Lampedusa's novel, which is set principally in the period between 1860 and 1862.

Gramsci's argument is that the entire movement toward unification was characterized not by revolution but by what he calls *transformismo,* "the formation of an ever more extensive ruling class." This notion is given the starkest narrative realization in *The Leopard* when, after fighting with Garibaldi, Tancredi quits the redshirts and joins the new Piedmontese army, which in turn launches an attack on Garibaldi and his men. During the ball scene a certain Colonel Pallavicino is an honored guest, much cooed over by the ladies: it immediately transpires that he too is a turncoat who actually went so far as to shoot Garibaldi in the foot at Aspromonte. Tancredi's opportunism will later go still further, since after marrying Angelica and making use of her father's money, he will become a senator in the new state, an honor refused by the prince. Tancredi's political views are perfectly encapsulated in his observation that "if we want things to stay as they are, things will have to change."[9]

It is difficult to know whether Lampedusa in fact read Gramsci's extensive analysis of the Southern Question (David Gilmour implies that he knew *The Prison Notebooks*), but clearly in many ways the two men's views are close. One of the earliest scenes in the novel is a visit that Don Fabrizio pays to the Bourbon king of Naples (the last of "this monarchy which bore the marks of death upon its face" [TL 19]). Despite the court's unattractive and clearly decaying ambiance, Fabrizio remains correctly courteous to his king, dutifully going through the forms of obeisance and deference that he feels are still required of him. Visconti removed the scene from the film, perhaps because showing the prince so reduced in authority might have compromised his romantic stature. In any event, Lampedusa's depiction of a South controlled up to 1860 by a decrepit and almost idiotic Bourbon kinglet, its lands arid, its peasantry poverty-stricken, its aristocrats decaying and hanging on quite hopelessly—all this conveys much the same overwhelmingly depressing atmosphere of ossification and local impotence that Gramsci also describes. Moreover the prince is also a distinguished astronomer; Lampedusa even invents a prize in astronomy given by the Sorbonne for his protagonist, and although it is a tiny detail, it consolidates the Gramscian notion of southern men of culture who stand out for their international achievements and enormous erudition but are unproductive so far as their own environments are concerned.

Social disintegration, the failure of revolution, and a sterile and unchanging South are evident on every page of the novel.

Yet what quite deliberately is not in the novel is a solution to the Southern Question of the kind proposed by Gramsci. Gramsci's essay suggests that the South's miserable condition could be remedied if there were some way to connect the northern proletariat with the southern peasants, to bring these two geographically distant, socially oppressed groups together in a common enterprise. Against the obvious odds, such a union would offer hope, innovation, and genuine change; and the South would no longer embody that disintegration which Lampedusa's novel so powerfully presents.

Yet so insistently does Lampedusa negate the Gramscian diagnosis and prescription—over and above the references to death, decay, and decrepitude on almost every page—that it is difficult not to assume that the novel is designed as an enormous obstacle to the alleviation of southern disarray. The paradox is that these late-style negations are conveyed in a thoroughly readable form: Lampedusa is no Adorno or Beethoven, whose late styles undermine our pleasure, actively eluding any attempt at easy understanding.

Politically, Lampedusa is almost totally anti-Gramsci: the prince stands for a pessimism of the intelligence and a pessimism of the will. The very first words in the novel are the concluding words of the daily rosary intoned by Father Pirrone—"*nunc et in hora mortis nostrae*"—and they set the tone of the entire book. The first event Lampedusa describes is the discovery of a dead soldier in the garden. Now is the hour of death, so far as the prince is concerned, since virtually nothing he does in the course of this work has any effect on the paralysis and decay that envelop him, his family, and his class. In short, *The Leopard* is a southern answer to the Southern Question, without synthesis, transcendence, or hope. "The Sicilians," Don Fabrizio tells Chevalley, the emissary from Turin who asks him to accept a seat in the Senate, never want to improve for the simple reason that they think themselves perfect; their vanity is stronger than their misery; every invasion by outsiders, whether so by origin or, if Sicilian, by independence of spirit, upsets their illusion of achieved perfection, risks disturbing their satisfied waiting for nothing; having been trampled on by a dozen different peoples, they think they have an imperial past which gives them a right to a grand funeral.

Do you really think, Chevalley, that you are the first who has hoped to canalise Sicily into the flow of universal history? [The prince speaks of various powers who have tried.] . . . And who knows now what happened to them all! Sicily wanted to sleep in spite of their invocations; for why should she listen to them if she herself is rich, if she's wise, if she's civilized, if she's honest, if she's admired and envied by all, if, in a word, she is perfect? (TL 171–72)

Whatever is melioristic, whatever promises development and real change, is dismissed as outside interference. (The prince is withering on the general subject of human perfectibility as advocated by Proudhon and by Marx, to whom he refers as "a German Jew whose name I have forgotten.") The Sicilian sun mercilessly beating down, the arid hills and wide fields, the imposing castles and decaying battlements are immutable facts, and it is those, not the political efforts envisaged by Gramsci, that have stamped Sicilian society.

And yet this ascetic philosophy sits alongside a love of life and a habit of comfort that are deeply ingrained. The contrast is starker, and yet—for a while at least—paradoxically more manageable in Tancredi, whose aristocratic bearing and immense poise derive from his uncle, at the same time that he yields more readily to Calogero Sedàra's daughter and the decidedly *déclassé* charms she radiates. The identification with

Sicily is the same in Tancredi, although his appropriation of the great southern island is basically predatory: "as if by those lovely kisses he were taking possession of Sicily once more, of the lovely faithless land which the Falconeri had lorded over for centuries and which now, after a vain revolt, had surrendered to him again, as always to his family, its carnal delights and golden crops" (TL 142).

The generations advance ineluctably, and as the old order represented by the prince dies, the social and political contradictions become greater, more difficult to contain or to render as personal history. The lateness of Lampedusa's novel consists precisely in its taking place as the transformation of the personal into the collective is about to occur: a moment that its structure and plot evoke superbly yet resolutely refuse to go along with. The prince cannot have a son succeed him; his only spiritual successor is his brilliant nephew, a young man whose opportunism and tangled exploits the old man accepts but ultimately draws back from. "If we want things to stay as they are," we have already heard Tancredi saying to his disapproving uncle, "they will have to change." Tancredi is very much like Napoleon's nephew in Marx's *Eighteenth Brumaire,* a man whose ascendancy depends on the exploitation of a class of people like Tancredi's father-in-law, Calogero: people who want the association with aristocracy as an entrée to power. The prince's other, and in some ways more authentic, heir is his rigid daughter Concetta, who cannot—even half a century later—forgive Tancredi's lack of delicacy and respect for the Church. Though she outlives her father and Tancredi, she has neither the intelligence nor the extraordinary, almost abstract self-esteem that the old Leopard has. Lampedusa treats her harshly. Her fondest possession is her father's dog, stuffed after its death, and the novel ends with her sudden discovery of the "inner emptiness" that the dog skin symbolizes:

As the carcass was dragged off, the glass eye stared at her with the humble reproach of things that are thrown away, got rid of. A few minutes later what remained of Bendicò was flung into a corner of the yard visited every day by the dustman. During the flight down from the window its form recomposed itself for an instant; in the air there seemed to be dancing a quadruped with long whiskers, its right foreleg raised in imprecation. Then all found peace in a little heap of livid dust. (TL 255)

A sudden, not to say catastrophically literal, decline such as this immediately raises the question of who or what Lampedusa is representing here. What and whose history is this, after all? Any acquaintance with the facts of the childless Lampedusa's quite uninteresting life impels one to assume that the novel is to some extent a Sicilian *Death of Ivan Ilyich,* which in turn masks a powerful autobiographical impulse. The last Salina is in effect the last Lampedusa, whose own cultivated melancholy, totally without self-pity, stands at the center of the novel, exiled from the continuing history of the twentieth century, enacting a state of anachronistic lateness with a compelling authenticity and an unyielding ascetic principle that rules out sentimentality and nostalgia.

Both the novel and the film problematically raise the question of history and once again the issue of genre. It is all very well to say, as I did a moment ago, that the novel is a response to and partial confirmation of Gramsci. Unlike Adorno's criticism or Strauss's late music, *The Leopard* presents no really difficult technical challenge and is readable, even conventional; yet it is, partly because of its circumstances and those of its author, a rare, that is, high cultural item. It resists generalizations almost as firmly as it resists pop sociology and was rejected by many publishers for its pains as well as for its limited appeal. Not so Visconti's *The Leopard*, which came into existence as a glossy super Technicolor film subsidized by 20th Century–Fox. When we read Lampedusa, we can have no doubt that this is a personal history and an idiosyncratic one at that. The novel allows us to ironize the prince when he speaks of and for Sicily. When Lampedusa reminds us in his own voice of the connection between nineteenth-century carriages and twentieth-century airplanes, we know that the house of Salina might, properly speaking, have ended, but its heirs did in fact live on after World War II, attenuated it is true but alive nonetheless.

Visconti's history of Sicily is also the history of twentieth-century films, from primitive fluttering images to an immensely powerful epic medium, whose bearer and self-conscious culmination, so far as post-Risorgimento Italian history is concerned, it is. The crowd scenes in the film, especially the Palermo street battles and the gigantic ball scene, testify to the prodigious powers of late-twentieth-century cinematic super-spectacles. The film's surface, no matter how carefully composed and modulated, is lavish, expensive, large, and at times overpowering. It makes one feel present as an insignificant onlooker with its amazingly detailed costumes, interiors, and outdoor settings, all of them authentic and above all luxurious. Nearly everything written about the film includes an account of Visconti's fanatically particular requirements—the one hundred tailors, the army of cooks keeping the ball scene supplied on a daily basis with meats and pastries, the fifty days of shooting and forty of editing for that one scene alone, the air conditioners and coaches and electricians and military consultants, and on and on. Lampedusa's intimate history of an aging aristocrat is suddenly blown up, made so explicit, that it becomes another story altogether, the collective history not of a diminishing family of Sicilian aristocrats but of modern Italy itself, rivaling Hollywood with its celebrities and magnificent scope. Visconti has said of his film that it is meant to be a realization of Gramsci's theory of *transformismo,* and this lesson is seen from the point of view of a prominent Left intellectual and aristocrat, Visconti himself. In fact the film is something still more—the collective account of southern decline as seen with the apparatus and power of representation of a northern industry, film, which is in the South so to speak not only to record the real Sicily but also to turn it into an object of enjoyable consumption.

A triumph of Guy Debord's *société de spectacle,* Visconti's *Leopard* is in effect a wonderful costume drama whose mastery of cinematic technique obliterates not only the privacy of the past but also its very pastness, its irrecoverability, which is at the heart of Lampedusa's novel. That work offers numerous insights into the past, but each of them leaves an impression of something unsayable or finally ungraspable. Thus when Calogero and Don Fabrizio are getting to know each other, the prospective father-in-law, crude but perspicacious, sees in the prince "a certain energy with a tendency toward abstraction, a disposition to seek a shape for life from within himself and not in what he could wrest from others. This abstract energy made a great impression on Don Calogero" (TL 128). The reader is afforded a number of insights here: into the prince's extraordinary self-sufficiency, his reserve, his fastidiousness and lack of greed, and above all his undiminished, if ultimately defeated, energy. Additionally of course Lampedusa tells us that Calogero was deeply impressed by this energy. And since the point of the whole passage is to suggest Don Fabrizio's "abstract energy" and his elusive inwardness, we cannot by definition get too much in the way of information or get very close to the prince. What gives the passage its heightened effect of lateness is that it is surrounded by many descriptions of mortality and decline, none of which actually affects or touches the prince's integrity, although he is a man whose time is over. Thus Lampedusa can suggest mortality and anachronistic heroism without specifying their precise nature, despite the fact that the prince is subject to the very concrete ravages of time and a public (because well-known) history of defeat.

None of this is even remotely possible in the film. Burt Lancaster's performance is, by any standards at all, a tour de force, a superb example of the film actor's craft. When the film was rereleased in 1983, Pauline Kael wrote an appreciative tribute to it in *The New Yorker* and went out of her way to stress Visconti's achievement in, for the only time she knew in film, describing the aristocracy from the inside. She has special praise for Lancaster who, she says very emphatically, commands the film's center of consciousness. "We couldn't be closer to him if we were inside his skin—in a way, we are. We see what he sees, feel what he feels; we know what's in his mind."[10] I think we can feel her enthusiasm for Lancaster's quite noble performance without really accepting any of this at all. The film exists aesthetically by virtue of the novel, but it does not, *cannot* reproduce the demanding ins and outs of character and circumstance provided by Lampedusa. Instead we get the pleasures of mimetic realism delivered to us in a visual medium that is far more specific about surfaces than Lampedusa's text. In fact, therefore, the film works not by getting inside but by moving outside the novel, distending, exaggerating, adding, and finally overwhelming its deeply pessimistic and private subject. It is not only by looking at Lancaster's tired face during the ball scene that we understand his stoical suffering, but also by cutting from his face to the overblown and yet deeply voluptuous sight of Angelica, and from Angelica to the amazing scene in what the script calls the *"galleria del poufs,"* where Lancaster seems so tired and overtaken by a sensation that looks perilously close to nausea as he gazes at all those women disporting themselves like so many ants swarming all over a piece of sugar. (Lampedusa actually describes them as "a hundred female monkeys" and the prince as "a keeper in a zoo" [TL 205]).

Similarly Angelica's laugh—overblown, loud, excessively long—when she attends her first dinner in Donnafugata as a guest of the Salinas: this pulls the film out from the private and abstract world of the prince into another realm entirely. There is something almost misogynistic about these scenes that I find quite disturbing. Visconti also adds an encounter between Lancaster and a serving girl en route to Donnafugata that isn't in the novel at all; and he embellishes with baroque interiors Fabrizio's nocturnal adventure into Palermo to visit Mariannina, the prostitute he occasionally frequents.

What Visconti uses film to do to the Lampedusa novel is to add to it a sort of cinematically Proustian descant, the fin-de-siècle concern with overabundance, the leisure and excessive pleasure of the privileged classes who do not give much thought to how much things cost or how long their money will last. Lampedusa's accounts of the prince and his family stress the impending poverty of this once-majestic aristocratic house; Tancredi is virtually penniless, and when Father Pirrone comes to remind the prince that Concetta loves Tancredi, the prince dismisses the thought because his nephew will need more money than Concetta will ever have. In the film Lancaster's expostulation is unprepared for, is in fact the one and only time in the film that we are given an indication of how desperately short the Salinas are of money. Even so, it goes by quickly, and Burt Lancaster's rendition of the speech suggests that he is as interested in living through Tancredi vicariously as he is in supplying him with much-needed funds. The rest of the time Visconti's film exudes unlimited wealth and undiminished prestige. The family retainers are silent servitors, the townspeople are depicted in effect as peons who exist to give obeisance, and when we get to the ball scene, one is given the impression that far from being a poor southern province, Sicily might as well be Paris.

As I said earlier, Visconti's *Leopard* began the last phase of his career, the first in a series of films concerned with a world that is both larger than life and irremediably, fatally decadent. This was also the period when Visconti was very involved in the production of opera and, insofar as we can impose a pattern on them retrospectively, lurid and melodramatic plays (like *'Tis Pity She's a Whore*). There is little of this sliding into destruction and sordid degeneration in *The Leopard,* which Visconti kept very carefully within the bounds of the heroic, the admirable, and of course the opulent. To a great degree Visconti is restrained by the nature of Lampedusa's novel itself, with its often mourning and certainly unexhilarating tone. Nowell-Smith opines that the ending of the film is also meant to be an ironic comment on the failure of Risorgimento, since while the Garibaldian rebels must die (there is a distant echo of gunfire), the prince and his family have made an alliance with the new class that guarantees their survival. He goes on to add that Visconti's own identification with the prince as detached from his family and Sicily—our last glimpse of him as he walks alone toward the sea—is balanced by "summary gesture" at most, since Visconti's reference to the failed revolution (the soundtrack gunfire) envelops the lonely prince and "gives the film a political perspective it seemed to have lost. But it is [only] . . . a homage to the revolutionary causes in which Visconti believes but is not involved."[11]

However one analyzes the politics of these two extraordinary works, it is clear, I believe, that politics are not really the issue: in both film and novel we have the reconstruction of an irrecoverable world, part fantasy and part history, dominated by a heroic figure of larger-than-life proportions. Neither work, in other words, allows us to identify with the Leopard, perhaps because most readers and viewers are those very same jackals, hyenas, and sheep of which he speaks to Chevalley, but partly also because the distancing effects of the colossal film and the subtly reflective novel conspire each in its own way to hold the reader/spectator at arm's length. In the novel Lampedusa underscores Don Fabrizio's patriarchal authority as keeper of his estates and of his family, the paterfamilias responsible for the welfare, and for its past, of his dependents. The fact that he is to some degree a real person, ancestor of the author who writes about them all with such tact and understanding, underscores his presciently dynastic gaze. There is a partial equivalent for that sense of coherence and responsibility in the film, but it does not derive from the character of the prince, whose authority and aura are, I think, very derivative from every other costume film that was made. (The character of the great lord, king, hero, and so forth is embodied in Hollywood film epics, from *The Sign of the Cross* to *Quo Vadis, Ben Hur, El Cid,* and *The Ten Commandments:* certainly Burt Lancaster brings that past with him. Interestingly, Visconti originally had wanted Laurence Olivier for the part, and then Marlon Brando, before he finally settled on Lancaster as star and as protégé of 20th Century–Fox). No, the prince's authority derives from the world put on the screen by Visconti, a world of which he, as director, is author. Qualitatively, of course, Visconti's world is a variant of that of the Lampedusa family, and because of its taste, scrupulous fidelity to nineteenth-century Italy, and superior cinematic intelligence it is not in the end a Hollywood film at all but the work of a late-style artist indebted to aspects of Wagner, Proust, and of course Lampedusa himself.

All this sits uneasily with the mass-consumer forms in which both Visconti and Lampedusa work. The contrast with Adorno, and even with Strauss, is very striking, since both of them worked in far more specialized and basically resistant media, the philosophical essay and classical music. In all four, however, one has a sense not just of a certain profligacy, a desire to go the whole way toward extravagance, and an arrogant negation of what is acceptable or easy but also of a very risky yet adversarial pact with authoritarian systems, not least of which is the authority of the imperious author, whose innermost characteristic seems to be to elude system entirely. Each of the figures I have discussed here makes of lateness or untimeliness, and a vulnerable maturity, a platform for alternative and unregimented modes of subjectivity, at the same time that each—like the late Beethoven—has a lifetime of technical effort and preparation. Adorno, Strauss, Lampedusa, and Visconti—like Glenn Gould and Jean Genet—play off the great totalizing codes of twentieth-century Western culture and cultural diffusion: the music business, publishing, film, journalism. The one thing that is difficult to find in their work is embarrassment, even though they are egregiously self-conscious and supreme technicians. It is as if having achieved age, they want none of its supposed serenity or maturity, or any of its amiability or official ingratiation. Yet in none of them is mortality denied or evaded, but keeps coming back as the theme of death which undermines, and strangely elevates their uses of language and the aesthetic.

SIX

The Virtuoso as Intellectual

Only a few figures in the history of music, and only a small handful of performers, have had as rich and complex a reputation outside the musical world as the Canadian pianist, composer, and intellectual Glenn Gould, who died of a stroke in 1982 at the age of fifty. The small numbers may have something to do with a growing gap between the world of classical music itself (excluding the music business, of course) and the larger cultural environment, a gap that is much wider than, for example, the fairly close relationships that connect the world of literature with those of painting, film, photography, and dance. Today's literary or general intellectual has little practical knowledge of music as an art, has hardly any experience playing an instrument or studying solfège or theory, and except for buying records or collecting a few names like Karajan and Callas, does not as a matter of course have a sustained literacy—whether that concerns being able to relate performance, interpretation, and style to one another, or recognizing the difference between harmonic and rhythmical characteristics in Mozart, Berg, and Messiaen—in the actual practice of music. This gap is the probable result of many factors, including the decreasing frequency of music as a subject in the curriculum of liberal education, the decline of amateur performance (which once included piano or violin lessons as a routine part of growing up), and the difficulty of access to the world of contemporary music. Given all these things, then, a few names that have important currency spring to mind: Beethoven, of course; Mozart (mostly as a result of Salzburg and *Amadeus*); Rubenstein (partly because of film, partly because of his hands and hair); Liszt and Paganini; Wagner naturally; and more recently Pierre Boulez and Leonard Bernstein. There may be a few others, like the three tenors who are mostly connected to opera and publicity, but even such remarkable and central musical figures of our time as Elliott Carter, Daniel Barenboim, Maurizio Pollini, Harrison Birtwistle, György Ligeti, and Oliver Knussen circulate as exceptions that prove the rule rather than at the very center of cultural life, which is where musicians of such stature should be found.

The point about Gould is that he seems to have gripped the general imagination and stays there still, more than two full decades after his death. He was the subject of an intelligent feature film, for example, and has turned up often in essays and fiction in quite unusual ways: in Joy Williams's "Hawk," for example, and Thomas Bernhard's *The Loser (Der Untergeher)*. Records and videos by and about him still keep coming out and selling: his first record of the *Goldberg Variations* was included in a list of the century's ten best recordings by *Gramophone* magazine, and a steady number of biographies, studies, and analyses of him as pianist, composer, and theoretician appear with noticeable attention taken of them in the mainstream, as opposed to specialized, media. To most people, he almost stands for Bach, more so even than extraordinary figures like Casals, Schweitzer, Landowska, Karl Richter, and Ton Koopman. It is worth our while, I think, to explore Gould's connection with Bach, and to try to understand how his lifelong association with the great contrapuntal genius establishes a unique and interestingly plastic aesthetic space essentially created by Gould himself as intellectual and as virtuoso.

What I don't want to lose sight of in these reflections, however, is that first and foremost Gould was always able to communicate a very high degree of pleasure not only in what he did as performer and personality but in the kind of intellectual activity his life and oeuvre seem endlessly capable of stimulating. As we shall see, this is in part a direct function of his unique virtuosity, which I shall try to elucidate, and in part also the result of its effects. Unlike the digital wizardry of most others of his class, Gould's virtuosity was not designed simply to impress and ultimately alienate the listener/spectator but rather to draw the audience in by provocation, the dislocation of expectation, and the creation of new kinds of thinking based in large measure on his reading of Bach's music. I adapt the phrase "new kinds of thinking" from Maynard Solomon's magisterial reflection on what Beethoven inaugurated in composing the Ninth Symphony—that is, a search not only for order but for new modes of apprehension, and even a new system of mythology in Northrop Frye's sense of the term. Gould's distinction as a late-twentieth-century phenomenon—his years of activity, including the period after he left the concert platform in 1964, began in the mid-1950s and ended with his death in 1982—is that almost single-handedly he invented a genuinely challenging and complex intellectual content, what I have just called new modes of apprehension, for the activities of the virtuoso performer, which I believe he remained all of his adult life. I do not think, however, that it is necessary to know all this about what Gould was up to in order to enjoy him as so many people still obviously do: yet the better one can comprehend the general nature of his overall achievement and mission as an altogether unusual type of intellectual virtuoso, the more interestingly rich that achievement will appear.

Recall that the virtuoso appears in European musical life as an independent force after and as result of the exemplary careers of Liszt and Paganini, both of whom were composers and demonic instrumentalists who occupied a major role in the mid-nineteenth-century cultural imagination. Their major antecedents, contemporaries, and successors—Mozart, Chopin, Schumann, even Brahms—had themselves been important performers but always secondarily to their fame as composers. Liszt was the greatest figure of his times, but he was known principally as an astonishingly compelling, not to say gripping, figure on the recital platform to be looked at, admired, and marveled at by a worshipful, sometimes incredulous crowd. The virtuoso, after all, is a creation of the bourgeoisie and of the new autonomous, secular, and civic performing spaces (concert and recital halls, parks, and especially built palaces of art to accommodate precisely the recently emergent performer and not the composer) that had replaced the churches, courts, and private estates that had once nurtured Mozart, Haydn, Bach, and in his early years Beethoven. What Liszt pioneered was the idea of the performer as a specialized object of wonderment for a middle-class paying public. A great deal of this history is contained in a fascinating compilation of essays about the history of the piano and pianists, *Piano Roles,* edited by James Parakilas. And as I have written elsewhere, the modern concert hall where we go to hear prodigies of technical skill is in effect a sort of precipice, a place of danger and excitement at the edge, where the noncomposing performer is greeted by an audience attending the event as what I have called an extreme occasion, something neither ordinary nor repeatable, a perilous experience full of potential disaster and constant risk albeit in a confined space. At the same time, by the mid-twentieth century the concert experience was refined and specialized into a profound alienation from ordinary life, discontinuous with the activity of playing an instrument for personal pleasure and satisfaction, entirely connected to the rarified world of other competitive performers, ticket-sellers, agents, intendants, and impresarios, as well as more and more controlling record and media company executives. Gould was both product of and reaction to this world. He could never have attained his degree of eminence had he not had the services of Columbia Records and the Steinway piano corporation at his disposal at crucial moments in his career, to say nothing of the telephone company, concert house managers, intelligent recording producers and engineers, and medical networks he worked with all of his adult life. But he also had a phenomenal gift that functioned brilliantly in that environment and yet moved beyond it at the same time.

There isn't much point in going over the characteristics that made Gould the extraordinary eccentric that he was: the low bench, the humming, gesticulating, untoward grimacing and conducting he indulged in as he played, the strange liberties he took with composers like Mozart whom he disliked, and indeed, the odd choice of repertory that would include the Bach that he made uniquely his plus composers—like Bizet, Wagner, Sibelius, Webern, and Richard Strauss—not widely known for using the keyboard as their chosen medium. But there is no way of getting past the fact that from the moment Gould's recording of the *Goldberg Variations* became available, a genuinely new stage in the history of virtuosity was attained: he lifted the sheer mastery of playing before the public to an elevation, or call it a side road or deviation, of an unprecedented kind. What made his appearance more pronounced as a sort of original event was that he had no known precedents in the history of music (Busoni comes to mind, but as soon as one saw or heard Gould at work, the comparison with the Italian-German thinker and pianist would quickly and rightly be dismissed), belonged to no dynasty of teachers or national schools, and played repertory (for example, Byrd, Sweelinck, and Gibbons) that had never been thought of before as furnishing staples on a piano recital program. Add to all of this Gould's remarkably fleet, rhythmically tense, and challenging method of playing well-known pieces, plus his core attachment to the fugue and chaconne forms that are perfectly embodied in the sarabande aria and thirty variations of the *Goldberg Variations,* and initially at least you have a totally unanticipated talent aggressing against the customarily placid and passive audience that has been routinized into the practice of sitting back and simply waiting to be served up a short evening's fare—diners at an evening's service in a good restaurant. A few measures of Gould's 1957 recording of the Beethoven Third Concerto with Karajan, or a scene or two from his video performances of fugue, tell us immediately that something besides concert virtuosity is being attempted here. It should be added that Gould's basic pianistic capacities were indeed quite awesome, certainly on a par with Horowitz's, who seems to have been the one pianist Gould considered his overrated rival. When it came to rapidity and clarity of execution; a phenomenal gift for double thirds, octaves, sixths, and chromatic sequences; a magnificently sculpted portamento that made the piano being played sound like a harpsichord; a unique power for sheer transparency of line in contrapuntal textures; an unparalleled ability to sight-read, memorize, and play complex contemporary, classical orchestral, and operatic scores on the piano (see, for instance, his renderings of Strauss operas, voice parts and all), Gould stood very very high indeed and was easily on a technical level with artists like Michelangeli, Horowitz, Barenboim, Pollini, and Argerich. So one could listen to Gould and get some of the same pleasures afforded by the old-fashioned or modern virtuoso, even though my point is that there was always something more that he did that made him so thoroughly unusual.

I don't want to recapitulate a lot of interesting accounts and analyses of Gould's playing here: we have an updated version of Geoffrey Payzant's pioneering study, for instance; we have Peter Ostwald's sensitive psychiatric account of the sadomasochistic component in Gould's performing as well as affective life; and we have a fully fledged philosophic and cultural study by Kevin Bazzana, *Glenn Gould: The Performer in the Work*. All of these, in addition to Otto Friedrich's excellent biography, are fastidiously intelligent and faithful renderings of Gould's practice as something more than a performing virtuoso. What I shall propose, though, is an account of Gould's work that places him in a particular intellectual critical tradition, in which his quite conscious reformulations and restatements of virtuosity attempt to reach conclusions that are normally sought out not by performers but rather by intellectuals using language only. That is, Gould's work in its entirety—one mustn't forget that he wrote prolifically, produced radio documentaries, and stage-managed his own video recordings—furnishes an example of the virtuoso purposefully going beyond the narrow confines of performance and display into a discursive realm where performance and demonstration present an argument about intellectual liberation and critique that is quite impressive and radically at odds with the aesthetics of performance as understood and accepted by the modern concert audience.

Adorno's studies of the regression of hearing amply showed how impoverished those circumstances were, but in particular he anatomized the kind of *Meisterschaft* and domination associated in contemporary performance practice with the cult of the virtuoso musician. Adorno finds this virtuoso typified in the figure of Toscanini, a conductor, he argues, who was created by a modern corporation to compress, control, and streamline musical performance into sound that would grip the listener against his/her will. I quote the following short extract from "The Mastery of the Maestro" published in *Klangfiguren:*

> Behind his confident manner lurks the anxiety that if he relinquishes control for a single second, the listener might tire of the show and flee. This is an institutionalized box office ideal detached from people, which mistakenly sees in itself an unwavering capacity for inspiring the audience. It frustrates any of the dialectic between the parts and the whole that operates in great music and that is realized in great interpretations. Instead we have an abstract conception of the whole right from the start, almost like the sketch for a painting, which then is, as it were, painted in with a volume of sound whose momentary sensuous splendor overwhelms the listener's ears such that the details are stripped of their own proper impulses. Toscanini's musicality is in a way hostile to time, visual. The bare form of the whole is adorned with isolated stimuli that shape it for the kind of atomistic listening associated more readily with the Culture Industry.[1]

Certainly Gould's desertion of the concert platform in 1964 at the height of his career was, he said many times, his way of escaping precisely the kind of artificiality and distortion Adorno describes so trenchantly and ironically. At its best, Gould's playing style communicated the opposite of the atomized and desiccated musicality that Adorno ascribes somewhat unfairly to Toscanini, the best of whose Verdi and Beethoven performances had the clarity and lean interconnectedness of Gould's Bach. In any event, Gould eschewed distorted effects that he thought typified the requirements of a stage presence, where one has to catch and retain listeners' attention in the fifth balcony. So he escaped the stage altogether. But what was this an escape into, and where did Gould think he was going? And why was Bach's music so specifically central to Gould's intellectual trajectory as virtuoso?

We can begin to answer these questions by looking first at an address made by Gould in November 1964 to the graduating class of the University of Toronto. His speech was couched in terms of advice that, I think, really outlined his own program as a performing musician. He spoke to the young graduates of the need to realize that music "is the product of the purely artificial construction of systematic thought," the word *artificial* signifying not a negative but a positive thing, "that it does relate to an obverse" and is not at all an "analyzable commodity," but rather that "it is hewn from negation, that it is but very small security against the void of negation that surrounds it." He went on to say that we must be respectful, that is, take proper account of how impressive negation is when compared to system, and that only by keeping that in mind will the new graduates be able to profit from "that replenishment of invention upon which creative ideas depend, because invention is, in fact, a cautious dipping into the negation that lies outside system from a position firmly ensconced in system."[2]

If we allow for a certain confusion between various imperfectly deployed metaphors, it is possible to decipher the sense of what Gould is trying to articulate here. Music is a rational, constructed system; it is artificial because it is humanly constructed, not natural; it is an assertion against the "negation" or senselessness of what everywhere surrounds us; and most important, it depends on invention as something that involves venturing beyond system into the negation (which is Gould's way of describing the world outside music), then coming back into system as represented by music. Whatever else this description is, it is not the expected kind of professional counsel volunteered by virtuoso instrumentalists who perhaps would more likely be dishing out advice about practicing hard, being faithful to the score, and things of that sort. Gould is doing the difficult and surprisingly ambitious task of stating a credo about striving for coherence, system, and invention in thinking about music as an art of expression and interpretation. We should remember that he says these things after years of association with a particular kind of music, Bach's, along with which he had undertaken a long-standing, volubly stated, and restated rejection of what he called "vertical" romantic music, music that, by the time he began in earnest his career as a musician, had already become the highly commercialized and accepted staple of the piano repertory featuring the kind of manneristic pianistic effects that most of his performances (especially of Bach) avoided strenuously. In addition, his dislike of being in close touch with the march of time, his appreciation of out-of-time composers like Richard Strauss, his interest in producing a state of ecstatic freedom by and in his performance, his complete retirement from the ordinary routine of concertizing—all these added substance to Gould's unusual virtuosic enterprise offstage so to speak.

And indeed the hallmark of his playing style as he continued to produce it, in the complete privacy of the recording studios that he inhabited late at night, was first of all that it communicated a sense of rational coherence and systematic sense, and second, that for that purpose it focused on performing Bach's polyphonic music as embodying that ideal. Now it is not as easy as one may think to have seized on Bach (and dodecaphonic music strongly influenced by Bachian rationalism) and then made him the cornerstone of a pianistic career in the mid-1950s; after all, quite formidable pianists like Van Cliburn and Vladimir Ashkenazy skyrocketed to fame at the very same moment, and the music they performed with such éclat was furnished out of the standard romantic repertory of Liszt,

Chopin, and Rachmaninoff. That material was a lot for a young and in effect provincial Canadian pianist to have given up at the very outset, the more so when we remember that not only were the *Goldberg Variations* unfamiliar music, but Bach piano performance itself was extremely rare and very much associated in the public domain either with antiquarianism or with school exercises much disliked by unwilling piano students who thought of Bach as a difficult and "dry" composer imposed by their teachers as discipline, not as pleasure. Gould went much further in his writing and in his playing of Bach, asserting that an "ultimate joy" was contained in the effort to produce an "exuberant and expansive effort at re-creation" in performance. We had better pause here and try to understand the assumptions behind Gould's statements in 1964 and the kind of pianistic idea he articulated in his playing of Bach, and the reasons for choosing Bach in the first place.

There is first of all the polyphonic web itself that radiates outward in several voices. Early on in his work Gould emphasized that Bach's keyboard works were principally written not for any one instrument but rather for several—organ, harpsichord, piano—or for none, as in *The Art of Fugue*. Bach therefore could be performed as if in marked isolation from the rituals, conventions, and political correctness of the *Zeitgeist*, which of course Gould dismissed at every opportunity. Second, there is the fact of Bach's reputation in his own time as a composer and performer who was both anachronistic in his return to the old church forms and the rules of strict counterpoint, and daringly modern in his sometimes excessively demanding compositional procedures and chromatic audacity. Gould built on these things quite deliberately by presenting himself very much against the grain of normal recital practice: his stage manners were anything but conformist, his playing went back to a pre-romantic Bach, and in his unadorned, unidiomatic, unpianistic tone, he attempted in a completely contemporary way to make musical sound the material not of consumerism but of rigorous analysis.

A justly celebrated essay published by Adorno in 1951— "Bach Defended Against His Devotees"—formulates some of what I have been suggesting about Gould in terms of a contradiction lodged at the very heart of Bach's technique, namely, the connection or link between counterpoint or "the decomposition of the given thematic material through subjective reflection on the motivic work contained therein" and "the emergence of manufacturing, which consisted essentially in breaking down the old craft operations into its smaller component acts. If this resulted in the rationalization of material production, then Bach was the first to crystallize the idea of the rationally constituted work . . . it was no accident that he named his major instrumental work after the most important technical achievement of musical rationalization. Perhaps Bach's innermost truth is that in him the social trend which has dominated the bourgeois era to this very day is not merely preserved but, by being reflected in images, is reconciled with the voice of humanity which in reality was stifled by the trend at the moment of its inception."[3]

I doubt that Gould had read Adorno or even heard of him, but the coincidence between their views is quite striking. Gould's Bach playing bears the inflections of a profound—and often objected to—idiosyncratic subjectivity, yet is paradoxically presented in such a way as to sound clear, didactically insistent, and contrapuntally severe, with no frills. The two extremes are united in Gould as, Adorno says, they were in Bach himself. "Bach, as the most advanced master of basso continuo, at the same time renounced his obedience, as antiquated polyphonist, to the trend of the times [gaudium, or style galant, as in Mozart], a trend he himself had shaped, in order to help it [music] reach its innermost truth, the emancipation of the subject to objectivity in a coherent whole of which subjectivity itself was the origin" (BDA 142).

The core of Bach is anachronistic, a union of antiquated contrapuntal devices with a modern rational subject, and this fusion produces what Adorno calls "the utopia of the musical subject-object." So to realize Bach's work in performance means that "the entire richness of the musical texture, the integration of which was the source of Bach's power, must be placed in prominence by the performance instead of being sacrificed to a rigid, immobile monotony, the spurious semblance of unity that ignores the multiplicity it should embody and surmount" (BDA 145). Adorno's attack on fraudulent period-instrument authenticity is not to everyone's taste, of course, but he is absolutely right to insist that what in Bach is inventive and powerful should not be squandered or sent back to the sphere of "resentment and obscurantism"; Adorno adds that the "true interpretation" of Bach's work is "an X-ray of the work: its task is to illuminate in the sensuous phenomenon the totality of all the characteristics and interrelations which have been realized through intensive study of score. . . . The musical score is never identical with the work; devotion to the text means the constant effort to grasp that which it hides" (BDA 144).

In this definition of it Bach performance becomes both disclosure and heightening, in which a particular kind of inventiveness in Bach is taken up by the performer and reformulated dialectically in modern terms. The heart of this kind of playing is Gould's amazingly prescient and almost instinctive understanding of Bach's creativity as manifested in a kind of polyphonic writing that is both virtuosic and intellectual in the discursive sense at the same time. For a brief explanation of what I mean, I have relied on a study entitled *Bach and the Pat-*

terns of Invention published in 1996 by Laurence Dreyfus. In my opinion Dreyfus pioneers a new level of understanding of Bach's basic creative achievement and in so doing transforms our appreciation of what it is that Gould himself as performer was able to do. It is a pity that Dreyfus nowhere mentions Gould because the common element for both of them is the word *invention,* which Bach himself used and which Dreyfus correctly relates to a rhetorical tradition going back to Quintilian and Cicero. *Inventio* has the sense of rediscovering and returning to, not of inventing as it is used now—for example, the creation of something new like a lightbulb or transistor tube. Invention in this older rhetorical meaning of the word is the finding and elaboration of arguments, which in the musical realm means the finding of a theme and developing it contrapuntally so that all of its possibilities are articulated, expressed, and elaborated. Much used by Vico, for example, *inventio* is a key term for his *New Science.* He uses it to describe the *ingenium,* the ability to see human history as something made by the unfolding capacity of the working human mind; for Vico, therefore, Homer's poetry should be interpreted not as the sage wisdom of a rationalist philosopher but as the inventive outpourings of a necessarily fertile spirit, which the later interpreter is able to recover inventively by putting her- or himself back into the mists and myths of Homer's very early time. Invention is therefore a form of creative repetition and reliving.

This idea of interpretation and poetry as invention can be given a musical extension by looking at the special quality of Bach's polyphonic composition. His remarkable gift for invention in his fugal writing was to be able to draw out of a theme all the possible permutations and combinations implicit in it that, through skillful practice, he could make it undergo as an object presented to the composing mind, like the material of

Homer's poems, for skillful performance and invention. Here is how Dreyfus puts it:

> Rather than conceiving musical structure as unconscious growth—an aesthetic model that presumes a spontaneous invention beyond the grasp of intentional human actions—I prefer to highlight the predictable and historically determined ways in which the music was "worked on" by the composer. This intention to speculate on Bach's willfulness invites us to imagine a piece of his music not as *inevitably* the way it is, but rather as the result of a musicality that devises and revises thoughts against a resilient backdrop of conventions and constraints. . . . [W]hile it is true that parts and whole in Bach cohere in a way that is often just short of miraculous . . . I find it more profitable to chip away at musical "miracles" . . . pursuing instead Bach's inclination to regard certain laws as binding and others as breakable, to accept certain limits as inviolate and others as restrictive, to judge certain techniques productive and others fruitless, and to admire some ideas as venerable while regarding others as outmoded. In brief, . . . analyses that capture Bach as a thinking composer.[4]

Thus Bach's gift translated itself into a capacity for inventing, creating a new aesthetic structure out of a preexisting set of notes and an *ars combinatoria* that no one else had the skill to use so outstandingly. Let me again quote Dreyfus here in connection with what Bach was doing in *The Art of Fugue:*

> Examining these pieces from the vantage point of the many different kinds of fugal invention, it is striking how, within the context of a monothematic work, Bach was never concerned with providing "textbook" examples of the subgenres, which

might conceivably have laid out the disposition of each piece in an exemplary and justifiable order. Typically, he crafted instead a set of highly idiosyncratic pieces that show how very far fugal invention can be pursued in the quest for harmonic insights. . . . This is why the *Art of Fugue* pieces so often go out of their way to frustrate pedagogically-oriented definitions of fugal procedures at the same time that they assert the preternatural status of fugal procedures as a source of the most inspired inventions.[5]

To put it simply, this is exactly the kind of Bach that Gould chose to play: a composer whose thinking compositions provided an occasion for the thinking, intellectual virtuoso to try to interpret and invent, or revise and rethink, in his own way, each performance becoming an occasion for decisions in terms of tempo, timbre, rhythm, color, tone, phrasing, voice leading, and inflection that never mindlessly or automatically repeat earlier such decisions but instead go to great lengths to communicate a sense of reinvention and reworking of Bach's own contrapuntal compositions. Dramatically the sight of Gould actually doing and acting this out gives an added dimension to his piano-playing. Most important, as one can see in the early and late *Goldberg* performances that eerily frame his career— one at the very beginning, the other at the very end—Gould excavated the highly refined contrapuntal as well as chaconne structure of the work to announce an ongoing exploration of Bach's inventiveness through and by way of his own virtuosic realizations.

What Gould seems to be attempting here is a full realization of a protracted and sustained contrapuntal invention, disclosed, argued, and elaborated rather than simply presented, through performance. Hence his insistence throughout his career that the very act of performance itself had to be taken out of the concert hall, where it was limited to the implacable chronological sequence and set program of the recital order, and planted in the studio where the essential "take-twoness" of recording technique (one of Gould's favorite terms) could be submitted to the art of invention (repeated invention, repeated takes) in the fullest rhetorical sense of that term.

Among other things then, what Gould did with Bach anticipates what we are only now beginning to realize about his enormous and singular gift, a gift that more than 250 years after his death in 1750 can be seen to have seeded a whole generation of aesthetic children, from Mozart through Chopin, to Wagner, Schoenberg, and beyond. Gould's performing style, his writing, and his many videos and recordings testify to how well he understood the deep structure of Bach's creativity and showed also his consciousness of how his career as virtuoso had a serious intellectual and dramatic component as well, which was to carry on that kind of work in performances of Bach and other composers who were, in a sense, invented by Bach.

I find it particularly dramatic and even poignant that on some important occasions (i.e., his liner notes to the *Goldberg Variations* recording) he would refer to Bach's major work, the one he chose to make his own, as having a generative root, an "aptitude for parental responsibility," in spawning the great exfoliation of thirty variation-children. Gould himself struck everyone who knew him, as well as his listeners and posthumous audience, as being a singularly isolated figure, celibate, hypochondriacal, extremely odd in his habits, undomesticated in every sense of the word, cerebral, and unfamiliar. In nearly every sense Gould did not belong, whether as son, citizen, member of the community of pianists, musician, or thinker: everything about him bespoke the alienated detachment of a man making his abode, if he had one, in his performances rather than in a conventional dwelling. The discrepancy between his feelings about Bach's music as fecund and regenerative and his own unreproductive isolation is, I think, more than mitigated, and indeed is overcome, by his performing style and what he performed, both of which were resolutely self-created as well as anachronistic the way Bach's were. Thus, the drama of Gould's virtuosic achievement is that his performances were conveyed not only with an unmistakably rhetorical style but as an argument for a particular type of statement, which most musical performers do not, perhaps cannot, attempt. This is, I believe, nothing less than an argument about continuity, rational intelligence, and aesthetic beauty in an age of specialized, antihuman atomization. In his own semi-improvised way, therefore, Gould's virtuosity first of all expanded the confines of performance to allow the music being rendered to show, present, reveal its essential motivic mobility, its creative energies, as well as the processes of thought that constructed it by composer and performer equally. In other words, Bach's music was for Gould an archetype for the emergence of a rational system whose intrinsic power was that it was, as it were, crafted resolutely against the negation and disorder that surround us on all sides. In enacting it on the piano, the performer aligns himself with the composer, not with the consuming public, which is impelled by the performer's virtuosity to pay attention not so much to the performance, as a passively looked at and heard presentation, as to a rational activity being intellectually as well as aurally and visually transmitted to others.

The tension in Gould's virtuosity remains unresolved: that is, by virtue of their eccentricity his performances make no attempt to ingratiate themselves with his listeners or reduce the distance between their lonely ecstatic brilliance and the confusions of the everyday world. What they consciously try to present, however, is a critical model for a type of art that is rational and pleasurable at the same time, an art that tries to show us its composition as an activity still being undertaken in its performance. This achieves the purpose of expanding the framework inside which performers are compelled to work, and also—as the intellectual must do—it elaborates an alternative argument to the prevailing conventions that so deaden and dehumanize and rerationalize the human spirit. This is not only an intellectual achievement but also a humanistic one. And this, much more than the kind of electronic fiddling Gould often spoke about misleadingly as providing listeners of the future with a creative opportunity, is why Gould continues to grip and activate his audience.

SEVEN

Glimpses of Late Style

I

Any style involves first of all the artist's connection to his or her own time, or historical period, society, and antecedents; the aesthetic work, for all its irreducible individuality, is nevertheless a part—or, paradoxically, not a part—of the era in which it was produced and appeared. This is not simply a matter of sociological or political synchrony but more interestingly has to do with rhetorical or formal style. Thus Mozart expresses in his music a style that is much more intimately related to the worlds of court and church than is Beethoven's or Wagner's, both of whom emerged from a secular environment that was highly involved with the romantic cult of individual creativity, usually at odds with its own time by virtue of unreliable patronage, and with the transformed profession of composer, who was no longer a servant (like Bach or Mozart) but a demanding creative genius who stood proudly and perhaps even narcissistically apart from his time. Comparatively speaking, Mozart was not a social misfit, whereas of course Beethoven and Wagner were: original thinkers who challenged the artistic and social norms of their eras. So not only is there often an easily perceptible connection, say, between a realistic artist like Balzac and his social milieu, but there is also an antithetic relationship that is difficult to discern and formulate in the case of a musician whose art is neither mimetic nor theatrical. Beethoven's late works exude a new sense of private striving and instability that is quite different from earlier works such as the *Eroica* Symphony and the five piano concerti that address the world with self-confident gregariousness. The masterpieces of Beethoven's final decade are late to the extent that they are beyond their own time, ahead of it in terms of daring and startling newness, later than it in that they describe a return or homecoming to realms forgotten or left behind by the relentless advancement of history.

Literary modernism itself can be seen as a late-style phenomenon insofar as artists such as Joyce and Eliot seem in a way to have been out of their time altogether, returning to ancient myth or antique forms such as the epic or ancient religious ritual for their inspiration. Modernism has come to seem paradoxically not so much a movement of the new as a movement of aging and ending, a sort of "Age masquerading as Juvenility," to quote Hardy in *Jude the Obscure*. For indeed the figure in that novel of Jude's son, Little Father Time, does seem like an allegory of modernism with its sense of accelerated decline and its compensating gestures of recapitulation and inclusiveness. Yet for Hardy the little boy is hardly a symbol of redemption, any more than the darkling thrush is. This is quite evident in Little Father Time's first appearance riding the train to be met by Jude and Sue.

> He was Age masquerading as Juvenility, and doing it so badly that his real self showed through crevices. A ground swell from ancient years of night seemed now and then to lift the child in this his morning-life, when his face took a back view over some great Atlantic of Time, and appeared not to care about what it saw. When the other travelers closed their eyes, which they did one by one—even the kitten curling itself up in

the basket, weary of its too circumscribed play—the play remained just as before. He then seemed to be doubly awake, like an enslaved and dwarfed Divinity, sitting passive and regarding his companions as if he saw their whole rounded lives rather than their immediate figures.[1]

Little Jude represents not so much a premature senescence as a montage of beginnings and endings, an unlikely jamming together of youth and age, whose divinity—the word has a sinister sound to it here—consists in being able to pass judgment on himself and on others. Later, when he performs an act of judgment on himself and his little siblings, the result is collective suicide, which is to say, I think, that so scandalous a mixture of extreme youth with extreme age cannot survive for very long.

But there is ending *and* surviving together, and this is what I am chiefly discussing here. Among other figures, writers like Lampedusa, the Sicilian aristocrat who wrote only one backward-looking novel that interested no publishers at all while he was alive, and Constantine Cavafy, the Alexandrian Greek poet who also published nothing during his lifetime, suggest the rarefied, almost precious, but formidably difficult aesthetic of minds that refuse connection with their own time while spinning out a semiresistant artwork of considerable power nonetheless. In philosophy Nietzsche is the great prototype of a similarly "untimely" stance. The words *late* or *belated* seem acutely appropriate for such figures.

In an introduction he wrote for Rachel Bespaloff's *On the Iliad*, Hermann Broch speaks of what he calls the style of old age as follows:

[It] is not always a product of the years; it is a gift implanted along with his other gifts in the artist, ripening, it may be, with time, often blossoming before its season under the foreshadow of death, or unfolding of itself even before the approach of age or death: it is the reaching of a new level of expression, such as the old Titian's discovery of the all-penetrating light which dissolves the human flesh and the human soul to a higher unity; or such as the finding by Rembrandt and Goya, both at the height of their manhood, of the metaphysical surface which underlies the visible in man and thing, and which nevertheless can be painted; or such as *The Art of Fugue* which Bach in his old age dictated without having a concrete instrument in mind, because what he had to express was either beneath or beyond the audible surface of music.[2]

II

Euripides is a strange combination of lateness, perhaps even decadence, in style and primitivism in content. He is more elusive in his values than the granitic Aeschylus, less sharp in his oppositions than Sophocles. Nietzsche characterized Euripides as the man who seized on the myth of Dionysus and Apollo—the foundation of the tragic form—rescuing it one last time from "the stern, intelligent eyes of an orthodox dogmatism" in order to make use of it again for tragedy. "What was your wish, sacrilegious Euripides, when you tried to force that dying myth into your service once more? It died beneath your violent hands: and then you needed a counterfeit, masked myth which . . . could only deck itself out in the old finery." In Euripides the old tragedy barely survives except as "a monument of its miserable and violent death."[3]

Strangely enough, Euripides' very last tragedies—*The Bacchae* and *Iphigenia at Aulis*—are works that self-consciously return in subject matter to some scarcely remembered beginning point, an early and yet profoundly disturbing clue to what Yeats called "the uncontrollable mystery on the bestial floor."[4] *The Bacchae* presents the advent of Dionysus, an Asiatic outsider to Mount Olympus, a god of uncertain but nevertheless menacing sexuality, who wreaks havoc upon Pentheus, the skeptical young king of Thebes who has succeeded Cadmus and now refuses to admit Dionysus as a god. The climax, told in an extraordinary speech by the Second Messenger, is that Agave, Pentheus' mother and a pliant convert to the Dionysiac cult, kills her own son in an ecstatic fit, tearing him from limb to limb. Convinced that what she has savagely mutilated was a lion, she then leads a procession of Bacchantes into the orchestra, bearing her own son's head in her hands like a proud trophy. Not only is Pentheus' palace also burned in the process, but Thebes itself is changed utterly. Dionysus is triumphant but at a scarcely imaginable cost.

In the *Iphigenia* Euripides situates his drama at the point immediately prior to the Trojan War, just as the Greek armies led by sons of Atreus, the brothers Agamemnon and Menelaus—one the husband of Clytemnestra, father to Iphigenia, Electra, and Orestes, the other the husband of Helen—are about to embark for Asia but are delayed by a dead calm at the port of Aulis. Calchas the prophet has informed Agamemnon that only if his daughter is sacrificed to the goddess of Aulis will the forces be able to sail. Stubbornly committed to his military campaign, Agamemnon in the play proceeds to lure his wife and children from Mycenae to Aulis, pretending that the young Iphigenia is being summoned to a wedding with Achilles. Clytemnestra discovers that her daughter is, in effect, to be murdered and naturally resists; in her, as Euripides unfolds the drama of mother, daughter, and father, are visibly planted the seeds of resentment and revenge that will later propel

Clytemnestra not only to adultery but to the murder of Agamemnon, exactly those bloodily tragic actions that had furnished the action of Aeschylus' *Oresteia*. *Iphigenia* ends with the young girl's willing, not to say saintlike, self-sacrifice to her father's ambitions, even as she walks away from her grieving mother. "Dance," she says to the chorus,

Let us dance in honor of Artemis
Goddess, queen and blest
With my own blood
In sacrifice
I will wash out
The fated curse of God.
O Mother, my lady mother,
Now I give you my tears
For when I come to the holy place
I must not weep.[5]

Despite their awful, terror-filled action, these plays make the heart visible, as Marianne McDonald phrases it in her book on modern cinematic versions of Euripides. True, the lineaments of age-old myth are as easily discernible here as they are in both Sophocles and Aeschylus, but Euripides is much more the psychologist of the situation, more the exposer of guile and manipulation, more the ethnographer of victimization and self-delusion than either of his two great predecessors. Thus one does not feel at the end of *The Bacchae* and *Iphigenia* the same sense of reconciliation and closure often found in earlier tragedies. Partly because of his relative lateness, Euripides uses his plays to repeat, reinterpret, return to, and revise his somewhat familiar material; but the peculiar sensation of the Euripidean tragedy is its playfulness, if by *play* one has in mind the prolongation of effort, the disinterested and almost purely formal gestures he uses to elaborate, extend, embellish, and illustrate the tragic action. One senses in Euripides both a vital modern psychology and a quasi-abstract delight taken in configurations of characters, situations, and rhetoric.

This makes his work not less urgent and disturbing as a result, but more. When, after having devastated Thebes and the house of Cadmus, Dionysus discloses himself, there is, I believe, an appallingly unique force in his words of self-revelation, as if he is perfectly prepared to go on playing with, harassing, and finally destroying the mortals who have slighted (but not seriously wronged) him. Euripides is as much the poet of that sadism as he is the melodist of Iphigenia's victimhood, her advocate against Agamemnon's ghastly tricks and macho insistence. When Nietzsche said of Euripides that he rescued the old and dying myths only to destroy them, he meant not only that Euripides dared to humanize what was distant and nonhuman, but that he imparted a human logic—a structure of vitality—to gods and heroes who would have otherwise remained outside time and beyond place.

Theatricality and music are the elements in Euripidean tragedy most compelling to contemporary directors. Andrzej Wajda's 1989 version of Sophocles' *Antigone* was designed as a political commentary on the transformation of Poland by Solidarity. Despite their great power, such parallelisms are inimical to Euripides, whose late works stage passion and cunning as musical variations on each other. For her tremendously daring conception of *Les atrides,* the French director Ariane Mnouchkine used *Iphigenia* as a prologue to Aeschylus' *Oresteia.* The Théâtre du Soleil, a long and narrow shedlike structure outside Paris in Vincennes, was converted by her into a rectangular bullring, compelled at the same time to serve as a sort of Bayreuth where ritual, music, and astonishingly compelling stylized acting combine to represent the fall of a house, doomed by genealogy and temperament to horrific deeds.

The heart of Mnouchkine's conception was the chorus, eighteen to twenty dancers costumed alike, whether men or women, in robes, kneepads, and fantastic black, red, and white makeup. The settings and their provenance suggested a sort of anthropological, quasi-folkloric Near East; they danced in rows that seemed to have broken off from the circular order of a *dabke,* although Mnouchkine's dancers were much more athletic and brash than *dabke* dancers. Her actors and actresses were ecstatic lyrists, yet even their tremendous composition of gesture and language was outshone by the extraordinary Catherine Schaub, who led the chorus. Catlike, elusive, smiling, and secret, she summoned, badgered, and dared the chorus, as well as the actors, with daemonic recitations, yelps, and anguished cries. Only she, among the choric ensemble, spoke. Yet all in the end, even the sacrificed Iphigenia and her terrifying mother danced to the insistent rhythms of a percussion band (gongs, drums, cymbals, triangles, xylophones), punctuated by an occasional horn and, at the final moment, the barking of dogs.

Ingmar Bergman's production of *The Bacchae* was staged as an opera at Stockholm's Royal Opera House in contrast with Mnouchkine's *Iphigenia,* which was conceived as a ballet with strophic interventions. The music was by Daniel Börtz, a serialist composer of local reputation. Dionysus was played by a woman, whose beauty and gymnastic strength further underscored the god's polymorphousness and dynamic scope. Like Mnouchkine's, Bergman's involvement in the production was total; each of the choric Bacchantes, for example, was given a name, life history, and character whose particular individuality lifted the chorus from collective anonymity to personalized involvement. The lyric ensemble was broken only once, when Peter Stormare as the Second Messenger narrated the dismemberment of Pentheus in spoken, as opposed to sung, verse. Less a ritualized than a familiarized version of Euripides' great masterpiece, Bergman's *Bacchae* heightened the terror of destruction and sorrow with the sense he gave that each of the personages on stage had had the Dionysiac experience separately. As in his films, the impersonal and the heroic were transfigured downward, so to speak, into everyday lives and informal happenings.

These two revivals of Euripides did not in fact bring him closer, even though they were performed in modern demotic languages (French and Swedish). In both instances one felt that the director intended an alienating effect, as if to say that we should not come too near or identify too easily with characters so manifestly ravaged by the rarest of dark forces and dark hearts. And this also had the effect of emphasizing what was already strange and out of season about Euripides in 410 B.C., when these plays were first performed. He dramatized the intersection of myth and reality, one turning upon and challenging the other. The result is an extraordinary artificiality, performance declaring itself such, marking itself unmistakably for perturbed and awed looking and hearing.

III

The Greek Alexandrian poet Constantine Cavafy died in 1933. He wanted 154 of his poems preserved, all of them quite short by the standards of twentieth-century poetry, each an attempt to clarify and dramatize, in the style of Browning's dramatic monologues, a moment or incident from the past, either a personal past or that of the wider Hellenic world. One of his frequent sources is Plutarch; he also draws on Shakespeare and was fascinated by Julian the Apostate. Alexandria haunts his poetry, from the beginning to the end of his career. Among his earliest works is "The City," a dialogue between two friends, the first of whom (perhaps a former governor) bewails his fate as a prisoner in the unnamed but clearly intended Egyptian port city:

> *How long can I let my mind molder in this*
> *place?*
> *Wherever I turn, wherever I look,*
> *I see the black ruins of my life, here,*
> *where I've spent so many years, wasted*
> *them, destroyed them totally.*

The second speaker replies in accents of cold definiteness that mark exactly the narrow range and stoic impartiality of Cavafy's style:

> *You won't find a new country, won't find*
> *another shore.*
> *This city will always pursue you. You will walk*
> *the same streets, grow old in the same neighborhoods,*
> *will turn gray in these same houses.*
> *You'll always end up in this city. Don't hope*
> *for things elsewhere:*
> *there is no ship for you, there is no road.*
> *As you've wasted your life here, in this*
> *small corner,*
> *you've destroyed it everywhere else in the world.*[6]

It is not only the place that has captured the speaker, but the repetitive action to which his fate compels him.

Cavafy considered "The City," together with "The Satrapy," as the way into his mature poetry. In "The Satrapy," the speaker addresses a man who is thinking of leaving Alexandria to seek out a new post in the provinces under King Artaxerxes. Against the success he hopes to achieve, the fugitive from Alexandria is reminded that

> *You long for something else, ache for other things:*
> *praise from the Demos and the Sophists,*
> *that hard-won, that priceless acclaim—*
> *the Agora, the Theatre, the Crowns of Laurel.*
> *You can't get any of these from Artaxerxes,*
> *you'll never find any of these in the satrapy,*
> *and without them, what kind of life will you live?* (CP 29)

Despite its limitations, Alexandria—which E. M. Forster once described as a city "founded upon cotton, with the concurrence of onions and eggs, ill built, ill planned, ill drained"[7]— holds the promise without which Cavafy could not live, even though it would culminate in betrayal and disappointment.

Cavafy's poetry has a persistently urban setting, which brings together the mythical and—with its ironic, understated tone of melancholic disenchantment—the prosaic. But to locate Cavafy in late-nineteenth-century and early-twentieth-century Egypt is to be struck by how utterly his work fails to take note of the modern Arab world. Alexandria is either the anonymous site of episodes from the poet's life (bars, rented rooms, cafés, apartments where he meets his lovers); or it is portrayed as it once was, a city in the Hellenic world under successive and overlapping imperiums: Rome, Greece, pre- and post-Alexandrian Byzantium, Ptolemaic Egypt, and the Arab empire. Partly invented, partly real, the characters in the poems are seen at passing—though sometimes crucial—moments in their lives: the poem reveals and consecrates the moment before history closes around it and it is lost to us forever. The time of the poem, which is never sustained for more than a few instants, is always outside and alongside the real present, which Cavafy treats only as a subjective passage into the past. The language, a learned Greek idiom of which Cavafy was self-consciously the last modern representative, adds to the parsimony, the essentialized and rarefied quality of the poetry. His poems enact a form of minimal survival between the past and the present, and his aesthetic of nonproduction, expressed in a nonmetaphorical, almost prosaic unrhymed verse, enforces the sense of enduring exile that is at the core of his work.

In Cavafy, then, the future does not occur, or if it does, it has in a sense already happened. Better the internalized, narrow world of limited expectations than that of grandiose projects constantly betrayed or traduced. One of the most dense poems, "Ithaka," is spoken as if to an Odysseus whose journey home to Penelope is already charted and known in advance, so the full weight of the *Odyssey* bears on every line. This, however, does not preclude enjoyment:

May there be many a summer morning when,
with what pleasure, what joy
you come into harbors seen for the first time;
may you stop at Phoenician trading stations
to buy fine things,
mother of pearl and coral, amber and ebony,
sensual perfumes of every kind—

But every pleasure is meticulously specified in advance inside the speaker's utterance. The poem's closing cadences rediscover an Ithaka not as goal or *telos* for the homeward-bound hero but as an instigation for his voyage ("Ithaka gave you the marvelous journey. / Without her you wouldn't have set out. / She has nothing left to give you now"). This leaves Ithaka itself fulfilled and also denuded of promise, incapable of attracting or even deceiving the hero, now that the course of voyage and return has run within the lines of the poem. Bound into that circumscribed trajectory, Ithaka itself acquires new meaning not as an individual place but as a class of experiences (Ithakas) that enable human understanding:

> And if you find her poor, Ithaka won't have fooled you.
> Wise as you will have become, so full of experience
> you'll have understood by then what these Ithakas mean.
>   (CP 36–37)

The grammatical form of the phrase "you'll have understood by then" carries the poem to its ultimate clarification, all the while leaving the speaker, who performs no action himself, standing outside, apart, tangential. It is as if Cavafy's basic poetic gesture were to deliver meaning to someone else while denying its rewards to himself: a form of exile that replicates his existential isolation in a de-Hellenized Alexandria where, in his best-known poem, "Waiting for the Barbarians," waiting for a disaster to befall is an experience suddenly dissipated by the realization that "there are no barbarians any longer," whence the self-deprecating regret in the phrase "they were, those people, a kind of solution." The reader is offered an ambiguous but carefully specified poetic space in which to overhear and only partly to grasp what is actually taking place.

One of Cavafy's greatest achievements is to render the extremes of lateness, physical crisis, and exile in forms and situations and above all in a style of remarkable inventiveness and lapidary calm. Often, but not always, Alexandria's history provides him with such occasions, as in the great poem "The

God Abandons Antony," based on an episode in Plutarch. The Roman hero is addressed as he is facing the loss of his career, his plans, and now at last his city: "say goodbye to her, to Alexandria who is leaving." The speaker enjoins Antony to set aside the consolations of sensuality, with its cheap regrets and easy self-deceptions. Rather, he is summoned sternly to witness and experience Alexandria as an animated, disciplined spectacle in which he once participated but that, like all temporal things, now seems to be moving away from him:

> *as is right for you who were given this kind of city,*
> *go firmly to the window*
> *and listen with deep emotion,*
> *but not with the whining, the pleas of a coward;*
> *listen—your final pleasure—to the voices,*
> *to the exquisite music of that strange procession,*
> *and say goodbye to her, to the Alexandria you are losing.*
> (CP 33)

What heightens the effect of these stunning lines is that Cavafy imposes a strict, perhaps even terminal silence on Antony so that he can hear for the last time the exact notes of the "exquisite music" he is losing: the convergence of absolute stillness and totally organized, pleasurable sound is wonderfully held together in an almost prosaic, accentless diction.

Forster's description of Cavafy as "standing motionless at a slight angle to the universe"[8] captures the strange, ecstatic effect of his always-late style, with its scrupulous, small-scale declarations, which seem coaxed out of a pervasive obscurity. In one of Cavafy's finest late poems, "Myris: Alexandria, A.D. 340," the speaker attends the funeral of his charming former drinking companion Myris, a Christian who in death is being re-created as an object of elaborate church ceremony. He

suddenly fears that he was deceived by his passion for Myris
and runs away from the "horrible house."

> I rushed out of their horrible house
> rushed away before my memory of Myris
> could be captured, could be perverted by their Christianity.
>   (CP 164)

This is the prerogative of late style: it has the power to render
disenchantment and pleasure without resolving the contradiction between them. What holds them in tension, as equal forces
straining in opposite directions, is the artist's mature subjectivity, stripped of hubris and pomposity, unashamed either of its
fallibility or of the modest assurance it has gained as a result of
age and exile.

IV

Donald Mitchell has quite justifiably, I think, raised the question of whether Britten's *Death in Venice* can be regarded as
being in more than a chronological sense a *last* work. Moreover he presents convincing evidence that Britten did not
intend the opera to be his final and therefore summary statement about the genre. But, Mitchell concedes, it is a *late* testa-
mentary work nevertheless by virtue of its subject matter.
Britten's frail and even precarious health, the opera's com-
pressed and often difficult style, which Mitchell describes as
belonging to the genre of "parable art," and the catastrophe
that befalls Gustav von Aschenbach: these converge in Britten's
choice of the solitary figure of the German (but symbolically
European) artist, a brooding and celebrated author beset by a
"late" impulse to flee Munich for a new locale largely because

(in Thomas Mann's words) "his work had ceased to be marked by that fiery play of fancy which is the product of joy."[9] Within Mann's novella, Aschenbach's half-aware and yet inevitable voyage to Venice induces in the reader the sense that because of various premonitions and past associations (e.g., Wagner's own death there in 1883) and its own peculiar character, Venice is a place where one finds a quite special finality. Everything that Aschenbach encounters in the tale—especially that whole range of demonic characters, from his strange fellow passenger on the boat to the overly amiable barber—accentuates the feeling we have as spectators that he cannot ever leave Venice alive.

Mann's *Death in Venice* was published in 1911, and so within his oeuvre the work is a relatively early one, all the more paradoxical for its autumnal and even at times elegiac qualities. Britten came to it at a late point in his life and career: we know, as Rosamund Strode points out, that he had it "well in mind by 1965," although its completion and first performance took place about nine years later.[10] The striking thing about both the opera and the novella, though, is how extraordinarily much they beseech, yet also reject, a principally or exclusively autobiographical interpretation. Both deal with crises, challenges, and complexities unique to the artistic life, such as Mann and Britten certainly experienced. We know, of course, that for both men homosexuality energized their explorations of their own creativity as artists: neither opera nor novella shies away from this fact at all. More important, however, is that both works in effect represent the triumph of artistic achievement over the final degeneration and terminal submission to disease and to illicit (or at least unconsummated) and irrational passion to which Aschenbach arrives. The old man dead on the beach in both works represents a carefully distanced object—pathetic and sad, it is true—from whom author and composer have already departed; this, they seem to be saying, is *not me,* despite the numerous parallels and suggestions.

According to Dorrit Cohn, Mann accomplished this feat by means of a "bifurcating narrative schema" through which "the narrator [who is not Aschenbach] maintains his intimacy with Aschenbach's sensations, thoughts, and feelings, even as he distances from him more and more on the ideological level." Cohn takes the further step, however, of also separating Mann's narrator from Mann himself: "the author *behind* the work is communicating a message that escapes the narrator he placed *within* the work."[11] Unlike Mann, whose ironic mode undercuts any simple moral resolution of Aschenbach's experience, the narrator constantly employs a morally judgmental rhetoric, which some commentators (she cites T. S. Reed) want to associate with Mann's failure of nerve: having conceived the tale "hymnically," he now wants to resolve it "morally," with the result, says Reed, that the tale is ambiguous in a bad sense, uncertain of its own meaning, disunited.

Like Cohn, however, I prefer to view the novella's apparent moral resolution as answering to the narrator's own needs and not to Mann himself, who scrupulously maintains an ironic distance from the narrator. Quite plausibly Cohn asks us to think ahead to *Doktor Faustus,* another of Mann's explorations of the artist's predicament. Neither Serenus Zeitblom nor the narrator of *Death in Venice* is capable of having "created" Adrian Leverkühn and Aschenbach respectively.

Mann's "irony in both directions"—between himself and the narrator, between the narrator and the protagonist—is achieved by literary, narratological means not readily available to the musical composer. And I think this rather simple, indeed elementary realization must be thought of as constitutive of Britten's whole undertaking in *Death in Venice,* an *askesis* imposed necessarily on him in the transfer of the novella from one medium to another. His librettist Myfanwy Piper admits as much throughout her valuable chronicle of how she constructed the opera's "book" out of Mann's, the latter "a dense and disturbing," endlessly evocative, ambiguous, and referential text, the former a translation of "very elaborate poetic prose" in the forms of the stage.[12] Quite rightly she comments on how a great deal of what she did involved cutting, paraphrasing, and condensing. What resulted was a libretto specifically designed to be mounted in the theater as the staging of story *and* music together.

What the very skillfully shaped opera story jettisons is Mann's narrator, the mocking, moralizing, explicitly ironizing voice that both describes what Aschenbach does or thinks and tries to direct our thoughts about it. For example, as the protagonist wanders through the city (he has just uttered his "I love you"), the narrator refers to him as "our adventurer," and goes on to describe Aschenbach's unhinged behavior, all the while of course standing farther and (more disapprovingly) away from him. This particular device is not to be found in the opera. Indeed, according to Britten's early sketches, it was quite deliberately forgone: the original plan had been to provide a sort of external narrative for the opera by having Aschenbach appear at times to be *reading* from his diary (seeming like a narrator to stand back from the action), but this was changed into a sung recitative accompanied by the piano. The outer narrative dimension was thus absorbed into the music, submerged so to speak in the musical element and especially into the orchestra.

Another particularly interesting change concerns a very early moment in the novella. Aschenbach has already seen the exotic man in the mortuary chapel portico, which inspires him (the man actually says nothing) to formulate his desire to travel south. The narrator then describes Aschenbach's thoughts, noting the cautionary limits Aschenbach imposes on himself: "he would go on a journey. Not far—not all the way to the tigers."[13] The reference is to "the eyes of a tiger" gleaming in the hallucinatory vision stimulated in him by the exotic man. In the opera both the cautionary idea of not going as far as the tigers and the outer narrative frame are dropped. The exotic man speaks directly of "a sudden predatory gleam, the crouching tiger's eyes," as part of his injunction (again, a direct one) to Aschenbach to "travel south." Moments later Aschenbach sings of his resolve to go to "sun and south" where his "ordered soul shall be refreshed at last." This is preceded by a few questioning lines of doubt about whether he should break with his orderly life, which soon afterward he does in fact break with.

Here the opera seems immediate and explicit, where Mann's text is circumspect and even ironically devious, since it will be precisely the tiger's world—that of the exotic Orient—that finally overtakes him in Venice in the form of an Eastern plague. "Not going all the way to the tigers" is one of those odd bits in the narrative that might be a part of Aschenbach's interior monologue, or it could be something introduced by the ironically observant narrator. In reading it "normally," we rush past it, a tiny detail that is quickly left behind. The act of solitary and consciously imperative rereading, however, allows for moments of pause and return; we come back over the text, we make distinctions, we move forward and back, and occasionally we discover these instances of ambiguity and even instability, where words may belong in one or another level of discourse. The sequential temporality of written (and hence of read) prose permits, indeed encourages, this sort of inward nonsequential activity. *Death in Venice* is in fact a text whose density, range of references, and highly wrought texture requires a slow, extremely deliberate decipherment very different from a reading produced under the pressures of theatrical musical performance, with its urgent succession of recitative, scenes, arias, and ensembles.

On the other hand, compared with all other musical genres, opera delivers the largest amount of direct information to be processed by the audience. Words, notes, costumes, characters, physical movements, orchestra, dance, and setting: these hurtle across the proscenium directly at the spectators, who must make sense of what is happening even though the sheer quantity of material nearly defies absorption and understanding. Britten's *Death in Venice* also carries with it the considerable weight of Mann's novella, the knowledge of which is perforce present as the opera unfolds. So what we see and hear therefore is a complex simultaneity of memory and actuality, all of it dominated by the presence of Aschenbach, whose first words— "my mind beats on"—make explicit the ineluctable forward movement of his story. Mann's work interiorizes the action, whereas—by necessity, of course—Britten's exteriorizes it: Aschenbach's thoughts are always audible in the opera, to be heard and seen, whereas in the novella Aschenbach is above all *legible*, scripted in that odd to-and-froing between his own thoughts and those of the narrator that I mentioned earlier.

Despite their differences, however, both works in the end convey feelings of overpowering solitude and, also because in both works Aschenbach nowhere consummates his love for Tadzio, great sadness. Aschenbach's failure to possess Tadzio physically is contrasted with the enactment of actual physical intimacy that goes on between Tadzio and his friend-antagonist, Jaschiu. And as in the last scene Tadzio seems to wander out to sea, the now terminally infected Aschenbach— grotesquely perfumed, coiffed, primped—sits in his lonely chair passively watching him, then expires. This literal gap between love and beloved is maintained throughout *Death in Venice*, as if author and composer want to keep reminding us that although Aschenbach travels south, he does not quite make it to the tigers—that is, he never arrives at that wild, presumably unrestrained region where desires are realized and fantasies fulfilled. For both Mann and Aschenbach, Venice of course is where he ends up, a southern city but not quite a truly Oriental one, a European but most definitely not a really exotic locale. The question remains, however, both for Mann and for Britten, who sticks quite closely to his great predecessor: why not in fact allow Aschenbach to go the whole way, and why the choice of Venice in particular?

Aside from its immediate anecdotal association with Wagner's death, Venice carries with it an astonishing, formidably dense cultural history that is the subject of a remarkable book by Tony Tanner, *Venice Desired*. More convincingly than anyone before him, Tanner shows that Mann's city is the inheritor of a rich history of the nineteenth-century imagination: Byron, Ruskin, Henry James, Melville, and Proust located in Venice a special quality that drew to it "appreciations, recuperations and dazzled hallucinations," most of them capitalizing on the city's peculiar appearance and its decline, as well as its power for attracting *desire*. "In decay and decline," Tanner says,

> (*particularly* in decay and decline), falling or sinking to ruins and fragments, yet saturated with secretive sexuality—thus emanating or suggesting a heady compound of death and desire—Venice becomes for many writers what it was, in anticipation, for Byron: "the greenest island of my imagination." When Byron left Venice two years later, it had become a "sea Sodom." Venice had a way of turning on her writerly admirers as no other city does.[14]

Venice's reality as a city combines two extremes almost without transition: a glorious, unexampled, and shining creativity, and a history of sordid, labyrinthine corruption and profound degradation. Venice as quasi-Platonic sovereign republic; Venice as city of prisons, sinister police forces, internal dissension, and tyranny.

The special force of Tanner's book, which treats Venice synoptically in such a way for the first time, is how he demonstrates that despite the enormous diversity of his writers, a certain troubling consistency in Venice's image keeps recurring. One is (Tanner speaks here of Ruskin) how in Venice "the transition from gorgeousness to garbage [the city's two extremes] is swift indeed." He quotes the following passage from *The Stones of Venice:*

Venice had in her childhood sown, in tears, the harvest she was to reap in rejoicing. She now sowed in laughter the seeds of death. Thenceforward, year after year, the nation drank with deeper thirst from the fountains of forbidden pleasure, and dug springs, hitherto unknown, in the dark places of the earth. In the ingenuity of indulgence, in the varieties of vanity, Venice surpassed the cities of Christendom as of old she has surpassed them in fortitude and devotion; and as once the powers of Europe stood before her judgment-seat, to receive the decision of her justice, so now the youth of Europe assembled in the halls of her luxury, to learn from her the arts of delight.

It is needless as it is painful to trace the steps of her final ruin. The ancient curse was upon her, the curse of the Cities of the Plain, "Pride, fulness of bread, and abundance of idleness." By the inner burning of her own passions, as fatal as the fiery rain of Gomorrah, she was consumed from her place among the nations; and her ashes are choking the channels of the dead, salt sea. (VD 124)

This rapid oscillation between Paradise and Inferno, Tanner shows, is central to Ruskin's vision. How suggestive it is for *Death in Venice*! Clearly Mann and Britten both seized on and, each in his own way, reappropriated this *topos* for each of their works.

The second feature of Venice's image is the way in which the city is always written about from the outside (by a visitor from the outside) and is therefore *already* "grounded in an image which in turn was nourished by a textually based text. Venice is always the already written as well as the already seen, the already read." Thus Proust in a sense inherits Venice from Ruskin by reading about it, and in turn writing it, so to speak, in his own idiosyncratic way. Tanner remarks:

> Farness is all. In terms of Proust's novel, Venice (the word-name) both represents and is the indefinable and unconfinable pleasure of absence, a pleasure which is indistinguishable from pleasure deferred, or that deferral which is pleasure. Venice present is Venice lost. . . . But perhaps that losing is a prelude to another finding—a finding *again*—in another mode. . . . The pleasure of Venice is no unambiguous matter. (VD 243)

Mann belongs in this formation, too, using—or rather, causing Aschenbach to use—Venice as a distant place to return to, and to locate or find in it that immense reservoir of cultural memory contributed to by his predecessors; in addition, Mann's own work is a regaining, "a finding again in another mode," of the Venice lost through time and distance. Britten's opera is yet another prolongation or regaining of Venice, much more explicit than Mann's in that it is unabashedly based on an already-there literary text that Britten reuses to explore the peculiar splendors of the city in terms of an artist's coming to terms with his own inner (and dark) sensual impulses.

In a rather intriguing way then, for Britten Venice is approached from outside via another text very much in keeping with the artistic image of Venice so persuasively analyzed by Tanner; moreover, by virtue of its history of glory and degradation, it is a preeminently *late* setting for a mature opera, for which a crystallized, much-worked-over style conveys in itself an allegory (Mitchell's word is *parable*) of the artistic/personal predicament of coming to a place, theme, or style at a late period in one's life, coming there not as to Prospero's island but rather to an old, much excavated, extremely worldly place, visited *again,* as if for the last time. We must remember that the problematic of allegories, and even of parables, is that *what* they allegorize is always viewed retrospectively, the fable or allegorical narrative coming *after* an experience or theme that is conveyed by the subsequent performance, so to speak, in a different, more attenuated, and coded form.

I noted earlier that Mann's *Death in Venice* employs an ironizing narrative device to distance Aschenbach from the persona who recounts the story of his infatuation with Tadzio, and that Mann uses this persona to place even more distance between himself as author and Aschenbach, his character. Britten's composition, however, uses the Mann novella without these narratological devices. So while *Death in Venice* the opera allegorizes its German "original," it does so in what is in effect an actualized present, or operatic time, unfolding before us in Venice (except for the two scenes at the beginning of Act I that precede the orchestral "overture," entitled *Venice*).

Now unlike a literary text such as Mann's *Death in Venice,* the opera is a collaborative work; still, Britten's role was quite clearly the dominant one: the music he wrote takes up the libretto, devises a total aural vocabulary, and finally shapes the work's aesthetic existence down to its smallest orchestral and vocal detail. Venice, nonetheless, remains central to the opera, although it too is absorbed into the work's musical fabric, its unfolding and actual present. But its role is quite different from the one found in its literary antecedents. The orchestral prologue identifies the music directly with coming to the city, which is not only talked about before but presented, or rather enacted, as a sensuous part of what the audience sees and hears *immediately:* thereafter Venice is where we are along with Aschenbach. So Britten's music not only accomplishes the approach to Venice (in the first two scenes) but also overcomes geographical distance and gives us Venice as a musical-theatrical environment, minus ironizing narrator and self-conscious skepticism.

Britten's technique of using opera to provide direct and immediate nonironic identifications of the sort that Mann's narrative art struggles quite consciously to avoid is clearly seen, I think, in his instructions that one baritone was to play seven distinct roles, all of them kept quite distinct (albeit obviously related to each other internally) by Mann. Intermittently but unmistakably, Britten reminds us that Venice is the setting of the action. It too is seen to embody numerous, simultaneously present identities: the polyglot hotel clientele, its staff, the various Venetian characters encountered by Aschenbach, and so on. But Britten's Venice is also revealed to be the site of a divine contest or *agon* (prepared for in the games of Apollo that end Act I) between Apollo and Dionysus. Yet when Dionysus actually sings in his own voice, it is as an outsider ("the stranger god"), although his dream appearance occurs just after Aschenbach has allied himself with Venice's underground self: "the city's secret, desperate, disastrous, destroying, is my hope."

By this time—to be more exact, a scene earlier—the city itself has been invaded by an Asiatic plague, described in great detail by the English clerk at the travel bureau to which Aschenbach comes for information. What Aschenbach experiences in the opera is therefore an accumulation of identities (much as the single baritone accumulates several identities throughout the work), all of them anchored in Venice, Venice as glorious city of Christendom *and* City of the Plain, Venice as European *and* Asiatic, as art *and* chaos. So too does Britten's "ambiguous" tonal idiom deliver a European and an Oriental orchestra—polytonal, polyrhythmic, polymorphous. It is as if Britten's purpose in the work were to set himself a series of obstacles and even ordeals to go through in Venice, which its ambiguous nature, part Inferno and part Paradise, necessarily entails and from which Britten does not flinch.

I would then speculate that Britten's *Death in Venice* is a late work not only in its use of Venice as an allegory to convey a sense of recapitulation and return for a long artistic trajectory, but also in its representation of Venice as a site for this opera, as a place where—for the main character, at least—irreconcilable opposites are deliberately collapsed into each other, threatening complete senselessness. Tanner very aptly suggests that for Mann's Aschenbach, the music he hears in Venice is an antilanguage, an idiom completely given over to a disturbing, distasteful, and bestial assault on the clarity of consciousness and conscious artistic communication.

In his opera Britten does not have available to him a ready contrast between words and music, or between the textual and extra-textual, and therefore he devises a music for the opera that draws on his past work as well as on non-European sources. This music incorporates normally discordant elements (much as Venice does) into an eccentric—that is, unexpected and rare—amalgam whose purpose for Britten is that it allows him intimately, and at very close quarters, to explore the limits of the artistic enterprise, maintaining and even prolonging those opposites whose basic difference goes back to the struggle between Dionysus, the stranger, and Apollo, the luminous sense-giver. Thus even though the opera does not go as far as "the tigers"—to the eradication of all sense—it does not *resolve* the conflict, and therefore, in my opinion, Britten provides no redemptive message or reconciliation at all. When Aschenbach is forced to the limit of both his mortality and his aesthetic capacities, Britten presents his protagonist's fate as that of a man able neither to draw back from nor fully to consummate his desire for the beloved, yet elusive, object. And this, I would finally argue, is the essence of Britten's *late work,* which is perhaps most poignantly embodied in the space we see between the seated Aschenbach and the increasingly distant Polish boy. Adorno, as we have seen, calls such figures of nearness and distance both "subjective and objective. Objective is the fractured landscape, subjective the light in which—alone—it glows into life. He [the artist] does not bring about their harmonious synthesis. As the power of dissociation, he tears them apart in time, in order, perhaps, to preserve them for the eternal. In the history of art late works are the catastrophes."[15]

NOTES

INTRODUCTION

1. Samuel Beckett, *Proust* (London: Calder, 1965), 17.

2. Gerard Manley Hopkins, *Poems* (Oxford: Oxford University Press, 1970), 108.

3. Ibid., 100.

4. *Power, Politics, and Culture: Interviews with Edward W. Said,* ed. Gauri Viswanathan (New York: Pantheon, 2001), 458.

5. "An Interview with Edward Said," in *The Edward Said Reader,* ed. Moustafa Bayoumi and Andrew Rubin (New York: Vintage, 2000), 427. Further references are cited in the text as "ESR," followed by a page number.

6. Edward W. Said, *Musical Elaborations* (New York: Columbia University Press, 1991), xx, xxi, 93. Further references are cited in the text as "ME," followed by a page number.

7. Theodor W. Adorno, "Alienated Masterpiece: The *Missa Solemnis,*" in *Essays on Music,* ed. Richard Leppert (Berkeley, Los Angeles, and London: University of California Press, 2002), 580.

8. Stathis Gourgouris, "The Late Style of Edward Said," *Alif: Journal of Comparative Poetics* (Cairo) 25 (July 2005): 168.

9. Edward W. Said, *After the Last Sky* (London: Faber and Faber, 1986), 53.

10. Edward W. Said, *Humanism and Democratic Criticism* (New York: Columbia University press, 2004), 144.

1. TIMELINESS AND LATENESS

1. "Late Style in Beethoven" has been published more recently in Theodor W. Adorno, *Essays on Music*, ed. Richard Leppert, with new translations by Susan H. Gillespie (Berkeley, Los Angeles, and London: University of California Press, 2002). Further references are cited in the text as "EM," followed by a page number.

2. Thomas Mann, *Doctor Faustus*, trans. H. T. Lowe-Porter (New York: Vintage, 1971), 52.

3. Rose Rosengard Subotnik, "Adorno's Diagnosis of Beethoven's Late Style: Early Symptom of a Fatal Condition," *Journal of the American Musicological Society* 29, no. 2 (1976): 270.

4. Theodor W. Adorno, *Philosophy of New Music*, trans. Anne G. Mitchell and Wesley V. Blomster (New York and London: Continuum, 2004), 19. Further references are cited in the text as "PNM," followed by a page number.

5. Theodor W. Adorno, *Minima Moralia*, trans. E. F. N. Jephcott (London: Verso, 1974), 17. Further references are cited in the text as "MM," followed by a page number.

6. Theodor W. Adorno, *Critical Models: Inventions and Catchwords*, trans. Henry W. Pickford (New York: Columbia University Press, 1998); translation slightly modified.

2. RETURN TO THE EIGHTEENTH CENTURY

1. *The Glenn Gould Reader*, ed. Tim Page (New York: Knopf, 1984), 86.

2. Theodor W. Adorno, "Richard Strauss," in *Musikalische Schriften* (Frankfurt: Suhrkamp Verlag, 1978), 3: 578, 579. Further references are cited in the text as "RS," followed by a page number.

3. Michael Steinberg in *Richard Strauss and his World*, ed. Bryan Gilliam (Princeton, N.J.: Princeton University Press, 1992), 183.

4. Page, *Gould Reader*, 87.

5. Jane F. Fulcher, *The Nation's Image: French Grand Opera as*

Politics and Politicized Art (Cambridge and New York: Cambridge University Press, 1987), 1.

6. Donald Mitchell, *The Language of Modern Music* (London: Faber, 1966), 101–2.

7. Norman Del Mar, *Richard Strauss: A Critical Commentary on His Life and Works* (Ithaca, N.Y.: Cornell University Press, 1986), 3:466.

3. *COSÌ FAN TUTTE* AT THE LIMITS

1. Charles Rosen, *The Classical Style: Haydn, Mozart, Beethoven* (New York: W. W. Norton, 1972), 314.

2. Andrew Steptoe, *The Mozart–Da Ponte operas: The Cultural and Musical Background to "Le Nozze di Figaro," "Don Giovanni," and "Così fan tutte"* (Oxford: Clarendon Press, 1988), 208. Further references are cited in the text as "MDO," followed by a page number.

3. Michael Foucault, *The Order of Things,* no translator credited (New York: Pantheon, 1971), 209–10.

4. Ibid., 211.

5. Emily Anderson, *Letters of Mozart and His Family* (London: Macmillan, 1938), 3:1,351.

6. Donald Mitchell, *Cradles of the New: Writings on Music, 1951–1991,* sel. Christopher Palmer, ed. Mervyn Cooke (London: Faber and Faber, 1995), 132.

4. ON JEAN GENET

1. "Une Rencontre avec Jean Genet," *Revue d'études palestiniennes* 21 (Autumn 1986): 3–25.

2. Jean Genet, *Le captif amoureux* (Paris: Gallimard, 1986), 122; *The Prisoner of Love,* trans. Barbara Bray (Hanover, N.H.: Wesleyan University Press, 1992), 88. Further references are cited in the text as "LCA," followed by a page number.

3. Jean Genet, *Les paravents* (Décines: Barbezat, 1961), 130; *The Screens,* trans. Bernard Frechtman (London: Faber, 1963), 153.

5. A LINGERING OLD ORDER

1. Theodor W. Adorno, "Alienated Masterpiece," in *Essays on Music*, 575.

2. Ibid., 577, 578, 579.

3. Theodor W. Adorno, "The Essay as Form," in *Notes to Literature*, trans. Shierry Weber Nicholsen (New York: Columbia University Press, 1991), 1:22–23.

4. David Gilmour, *The Last Leopard: A Life of Giuseppe di Lampedusa* (London, New York: Quartet Books, 1988), 127.

5. Laurence Schifano, *Luchino Visconti: The Flames of Passion*, trans. William S. Byron (London: Collins, 1990), 434.

6. Gilmour, *Last Leopard*, 121–22.

7. Schifano, *Visconti*, 75.

8. Geoffrey Nowell-Smith, *Luchino Visconti* (Garden City, N.Y.: Doubleday, 1968), 110–11.

9. Giuseppe Tomasi di Lampedusa, *The Leopard,* trans. Archibald Colquhoun (London: Collins and Harvill, 1960), 31. Further references are cited in the text as "TL," followed by a page number.

10. Pauline Kael, *State of the Art* (New York: Dutton, 1985), 52.

11. Nowell-Smith, *Visconti*, 116–17.

6. THE VIRTUOSO AS INTELLECTUAL

1. Theodor W. Adorno, *Sound Figures,* trans. Robert Livingstone (Stanford, Calif.: Stanford Unviersity Press, 1999), 47.

2. Page, *Gould Reader,* 4–5.

3. Theodor W. Adorno, "Bach Defended Against His Devotees," in *Prisms,* trans. Samuel and Shierry Weber (Cambridge, Mass.: MIT Press), 139. Further references are cited in the text as "BDA," followed by a page number.

4. Laurence Dreyfus, *Bach and the Patterns of Invention* (Cambridge, Mass.: Harvard University Press, 1996), 27.

5. Ibid., 160.

7. GLIMPSES OF LATE STYLE

1. Thomas Hardy, *Jude the Obscure* (London and New York: Penguin, 1998), 342–43.

2. Hermann Broch, "Introduction," in Rachel Bespaloff, *On the Iliad,* trans. Mary McCarthy (New York: Pantheon, 1947), 10.

3. Friedrich Nietzsche, *The Birth of Tragedy,* trans. Shaun Whiteside (New York and London: Penguin, 1993), 54–55.

4. W. B. Yeats, "The Magi," in *Collected Poems* (New York: Scribner, 1996), 126.

5. Euripides, *Iphigenia in Aulis,* trans. Charles R. Walker, in *Euripides* (New York: Modern Library, n.d.), 3:194.

6. C. P. Cavafy, "The City," in *Collected Poems,* trans. Edmund Keeley and Philip Sherrard (Princeton, N.J.: Princeton University Press, 1992), 28. Further references are cited in the text as "CP," followed by a page number.

7. E. M. Forster, "The Poetry of C. P. Cavafy," in *Pharos and Pharillon* (New York: Knopf, 1962), 91.

8. Ibid.

9. Thomas Mann, *Death in Venice,* in *Death in Venice and Seven Other Stories,* trans. H. T. Lowe-Porter (New York: Vintage, 1954), 7.

10. Rosamund Strode, "A Death in Venice Chronicle," in *Benjamin Britten: Death in Venice,* ed. Donald Mitchell (Cambridge, Mass.: Cambridge University Press, 1987), 26.

11. Dorrit Cohn, "The Second Author of *Der Tod in Venedig,*" in *Critical Essays on Thomas Mann,* ed. Inta M. Ezergailis (Boston: G. K. Hall & Co., 1988), 126.

12. Myfanwy Piper, "The Libretto," in *Benjamin Britten,* 50.

13. Mann, *Death in Venice,* 8.

14. Tony Tanner, *Venice Desired* (Oxford, U.K.: Blackwell, 1992), 5. Further references are cited in the text as "VD," followed by a page number.

15. Adorno, *Essays in Music,* 567.

INDEX

ABOUT THE AUTHOR

Edward W. Said was University Professor of English and Comparative Literature at Columbia University. He was the author of more than twenty books, including *Orientalism* and *Culture and Imperialism,* and his essays and reviews appeared in newspapers and periodicals throughout the world. Said died in September 2003.

A NOTE ON THE TYPE

The text of this book was set in Sabon, a typeface designed by Jan Tschichold (1902–1974), the well-known German typographer. Based loosely on the original designs by Claude Garamond (c. 1480–1561), Sabon is unique in that it was explicitly designed for hotmetal composition on both the Monotype and Linotype machines as well as for filmsetting. Designed in 1966 in Frankfurt, Sabon was named for the famous Lyons punch cutter Jacques Sabon, who is thought to have brought some of Garamond's matrices to Frankfurt.

Composed by Creative Graphics,
Allentown, Pennsylvania
Printed and bound by R. R. Donnelley & Sons,
Harrisonburg, Virginia
Designed by M. Kristen Bearse